Breads
for Beginners

Publications International, Ltd.

Microwave Cooking: Microwave ovens vary in wattage. Use the cooking times as guidelines and check for doneness before adding more time.

WARNING: Food preparation, baking and cooking involve inherent dangers: misuse of electric products, sharp electric tools, boiling water, hot stoves, allergic reactions, foodborne illnesses and the like, pose numerous potential risks. Publications International, Ltd. (PIL) assumes no responsibility or liability for any damages you may experience as a result of following recipes, instructions, tips or advice in this publication.

While we hope this publication helps you find new ways to eat delicious foods, you may not always achieve the results desired due to variations in ingredients, cooking temperatures, typos, errors, omissions or individual cooking abilities.

Let's get social!

 @Publications_International

 @PublicationsInternational

www.pilbooks.com

Contents

Bread Baking Basics

Who can resist the temptation of homemade bread? From sweet and savory quick breads and muffins to simple sandwich breads and hearty whole grain breads, a fresh-from-the-oven loaf is always an irresistible treat. And it's something that everyone, including beginners, can make at home—you don't need to buy expensive ingredients or invest in special equipment to make good bread. If you always thought baking bread was too complicated or time-consuming, this is the book for you.

Getting Started

The world of bread is a big one, so start out with the basics and you won't be overwhelmed. Quick breads are the simplest to make, and as the name suggests, they are quick and easy to put together. They contain chemical leaveners (baking powder and/or baking soda) and require very little mixing or kneading and no rising time prior to baking. Yeast breads contain yeast as a leavening agent; they generally require stirring or kneading plus time to rise (both contribute to the structure, flavor and texture of the bread).

For the best possible results, read through the following information before getting started. These bread-baking basics, plus tips, techniques and easy-to-follow recipes will help you discover the joy of baking—and show you just how simple and rewarding baking bread can be.

Essential Ingredients

Butter: Butter imparts flavor, richness and tenderness to breads. Always use unsalted butter so you can control the amount of salt in the recipe. The temperature of the butter is important in many bread recipes; cold butter is required to make biscuits and scones flaky, while melted butter should not be so hot that it would kill the yeast or cook the eggs in a quick bread batter.

Flour: All-purpose flour is the most commonly available flour and the one used in the majority of these recipes. Bread flour is a high-protein flour; it produces more gluten and contributes to a more elastic dough and a higher rise. You can substitute all-purpose flour for bread flour, although the results might not be exactly the same. Several recipes in this book call for whole wheat flour and rye flour; these are more perishable than all-purpose flour and should be purchased in small amounts and stored in a cool place. These flours are usually used in combination with all-purpose flour to avoid overly dense or poorly risen loaves.

Oil: For many recipes, a neutral-tasting oil such as vegetable, canola or sunflower oil is the best option to provide richness to a bread without affecting the flavor. For Italian and Mediterranean-style breads, such as focaccia, pizza, cheese or herb breads, olive oil is often used for flavor.

Salt: Salt adds flavor to breads (both sweet and savory) and strengthens the dough, contributing to its final texture. It also slows the fermentation process in yeast breads, allowing the flavor of the dough to develop over time. Use regular table salt when baking bread, as it's simple to measure and dissolves easily. Special salts may be used for topping, such as coarse salt on pretzels or flaky sea salt on focaccia.

Sugar: Granulated sugar, brown sugar and other sweeteners (such as honey, maple syrup and molasses) feed the yeast, as well as add their own flavors to breads. They help produce a browner crust and improve the texture and tenderness in both quick and yeast breads while also helping breads retain moisture.

Yeast: Yeast is what makes breads rise—when activated by warm liquid and fed by sugar and starch, yeast slowly releases carbon dioxide gas bubbles that stretch the structure of the dough and causes it to rise. Two types of dry yeast are commonly available: active dry yeast and instant yeast (also known as quick-rise or rapid-rise). Both types are available in packets or jars and should be stored in a cool, dry place or in the refrigerator once the package is opened. (Be sure to check the expiration date before purchasing and using.) See page 9 for additional tips on using yeast.

Quick Bread Tips & Techniques

Chill Out

The butter or shortening in biscuit and scone recipes must be cold to ensure light and flaky results. Recipe directions call for cutting the fat into a flour mixture, which simply means that the fat is incorporated into the flour mixture without overworking or softening the butter or shortening too much. This can be done with a pastry blender, two knives, a fork or fingertips; the goal is to end up with small pea-size pieces or coarse crumbs (the recipe will specify the size) before liquid is added. A food processor can also be used to mix a biscuit or scone dough quickly, which helps keep the fat cold and results in lighter biscuits and scones.

Easy Does It

Don't overmix! Quick bread loaves and muffins are most commonly made with the quick bread method, which means combining the dry ingredients in one bowl and the wet ingredients in another bowl and mixing them together. This mixture should be stirred gently and as briefly as possible, just until the dry ingredients are moistened—you don't want to work the gluten too much or deflate the air bubbles that form from the action of the baking powder or baking soda. It's ok if the batter is lumpy. Too much stirring will give breads a tough texture and cause muffins to turn out dry with lots of holes and tunnels. Use a rubber spatula or wooden spoon to blend the batter only until no streaks of flour remain.

No Waiting

Unlike yeast breads which need time to rest and rise, quick breads (all types) should be baked immediately after mixing. The leaveners (baking powder and/or baking soda) begin to work as soon as the dry and wet ingredients are mixed together, forming carbon dioxide bubbles that make the bread rise. If baking is delayed, the leaveners can lose their power and you may end up with a flatter, denser bread.

Is it Done Yet?

The easiest way to check for doneness is with a wooden toothpick; when inserted into the center of a quick bread or muffin, it should come out clean or with just a few crumbs attached. Raw batter on the toothpick means that the bread needs a little more baking time. Biscuits and scones are done when their top and bottom crusts are an even golden brown color. It's best to check for doneness at the minimum time given in a recipe (or a few minutes before)—you can always add more time.

Hurry Up and Wait

While quick bread loaves should be baked soon after mixing the batter, most of them should be cooled completely (1 to 2 hours) before slicing to prevent crumbling. Smaller breads like muffins, biscuits and scones may be eaten after cooling briefly. Follow the specific cooling instructions in each recipe.

Yeast Bread Tips & Techniques

It's Alive!

Yeast is a living microorganism that is activated with warm liquid. Active dry yeast should be combined directly with a warm liquid (105° to 115°F) to rehydrate and proof the yeast—this means letting the mixture stand for about 5 minutes or until it becomes bubbly; this thin layer of bubbles on top of the liquid proves the yeast is alive. It's important to use liquid that's not too hot, as a liquid that is over 120°F will kill yeast. Use a thermometer to check the temperature if possible, but if you're testing the temperature by hand, the liquid should be warm enough to stick your finger in and hold it there comfortably. Active dry yeast is highly perishable, so check the expiration date before using and don't purchase large quanitites.

Instant yeast has smaller particles than active dry yeast, so it dissolves more quickly into the dough and does not require rehydration and proofing. Instant yeast is usually combined directly with other dry ingredients, and hotter liquids (up to 130°F) can be used in making dough. The two types of yeast are generally interchangeable with minor adjustments: To substitute instant yeast for active dry yeast, use about 25% less and add it directly to the dry ingredients; the rising time may be reduced by 10 to 15 minutes. To substitute active dry yeast for instant, dissolve the yeast in a small portion of the liquid from the recipe to rehydrate before proceeding with the rest of the recipe.

Knead to Know

Kneading is essential to develop and strengthen the gluten, a protein in wheat flour which creates the bread's structure. Kneading also incorporates and homogenizes the ingredients in the dough. Kneading is most frequently done in an electric stand mixer; most doughs take about 5 minutes and should be mixed at a low speed. Doughs can also be made in a food processor, which makes quick work of kneading. Or you can knead dough by hand; this takes a little longer to develop a smooth and elastic dough.

Whatever method of kneading you choose, you want to avoid adding too much flour. Dough always starts out very sticky so it's tempting to add a lot of flour to smooth it out, but this can result in a very dry, tough and crumbly bread. As dough is kneaded, the flour gradually hydrates, absorbing the water and distributing it more evenly which makes the dough softer and smoother. So it can take some time and patience to reach the end stage—but not always additional flour. And if you find that your dough is difficult to roll or stretch out after rising, sometimes just letting it rest a little longer will solve the problem.

In the cases of no-knead or low-knead breads (like the Rustic White Bread on page 108), the gluten in the dough is developed over several long, slow rises rather than by kneading. These doughs are wetter than traditionally kneaded doughs; they require far more time but much less handling.

Rise Up

Letting the dough rise means allowing time for the yeast cells to give off carbon dioxide gas. This process gradually expands the dough and develops its flavor, texture and structure. To prevent the dough from drying out, it should be placed in a greased bowl—you can use oil or nonstick cooking spray—and turn it over so the top is greased as well. Cover the dough with a clean kitchen towel and set it in a warm place (about 80°F) until the dough has expanded as the recipe directs (usually doubling in size).

Poking and Punching

To test whether the dough has risen enough, lightly press two fingertips about one-half inch into the dough. The dough is ready if the indentations remain when you remove your fingertips. Rising times given in the recipes are approximate; your times may differ due to the temperature and humidity level of your kitchen.

The next step is usually punching down the dough, which removes some of the gas bubbles formed by the yeast during rising and helps redistribute the yeast for the final proofing stage. Contrary to the name, punching should be done gently, first pushing your fist into the center of the dough, then pulling the edges of the dough towards the center and shaping it into a ball. The dough is now ready to rise again or shape, but if time allows, let the dough rest, covered, for 10 minutes before proceeding. This helps relax the gluten and makes the dough easier to shape or roll out.

The Burden of Proof

After rolling or shaping the dough, it's time for the final or second rise which is called proofing. The dough is once again covered and set aside to rest and rise, and the doneness tests are similar to the ones in the first rise: The dough should almost double in size, and an indentation will slowly fill in when the dough is gently pressed with a finger. Proof times may vary depending on the temperature of the room and the dough; the recipes will offer specific guidance.

The Wait is Over

Yeast breads are done when they are fully expanded and the crust is dry, firm and golden brown. It can be challenging to determine the doneness of yeast breads, especially for new bakers. Breads baked in loaf pans will pull away from the sides of the pan. You can tap the bread—thump the top or bottom of a loaf with your fingers or a wooden spoon—and listen to the sound it makes. A hollow sound means the bread is done; a dull thud means the bread is still moist inside and requires more baking. You can also use a thermometer to take the internal temperature of the bread. Insert the thermometer into the center (go in at an angle through the side or the bottom to avoid leaving a visible mark); most breads are done between 190° and 200°F, while enriched breads that contain eggs, butter and/or milk are done at about 185°F. When in doubt, err on the side of additional time—it's better to have a darker crust than an underbaked loaf.

Cool It

Letting yeast breads cool at least 30 minutes in most cases is essential—cooling sets the crumb and the crust. If you cut into them too soon, they will be difficult to slice, the bread will be gummy and the slices won't hold their shape. Breads baked in loaf pans should be removed from the pans immediately after baking and cooled on a wire rack to prevent the crust from getting soggy.

Keepin' it Fresh

Most homemade breads will become stale within a few days since they contain no preservatives. Crusty loaves are best stored unwrapped at room temperature; soft-crust loaves should be stored in airtight plastic bags or tightly wrapped in foil or plastic wrap. If your kitchen is very warm and humid, breads should be stored in the refrigerator. (Refrigeration dries out the bread more quickly but slows the growth of mold.) Breads containing milk and fat will last longer than those containing water and no fat.

For longer storage, you can freeze your bread—wrap it well in foil or plastic wrap, then place it in an airtight freezer bag and freeze up to several months. And if you do end up with leftover bread, it's not a bad problem to have. Consider making bread crumbs, croutons, stuffing, stratas, French toast or bread puddings—they're all even better with homemade bread!

Quick Breads

Peanut Butter Chocolate Chip Bread

Makes 1 loaf

1½ cups all-purpose flour

2 teaspoons baking powder

½ teaspoon salt

¼ teaspoon ground cinnamon

⅛ teaspoon ground nutmeg

⅔ cup milk

1 teaspoon vanilla

¾ cup packed dark brown sugar

½ cup vegetable oil

½ cup creamy peanut butter

2 eggs

1 cup finely chopped roasted salted peanuts

1 cup mini semisweet chocolate chips

1. Preheat oven to 350°F. Spray 9×5-inch loaf pan with nonstick cooking spray or line with parchment paper.

2. Combine flour, baking powder, salt, cinnamon and nutmeg in medium bowl; mix well. Combine milk and vanilla in small bowl.

3. Combine brown sugar, oil and peanut butter in large bowl; stir until well blended. Add eggs, one at a time; beat until blended. Alternately add flour mixture and milk mixture in two additions, stirring just until blended. Stir in peanuts and chocolate chips. Spread batter in prepared pan.

4. Bake about 1 hour or until toothpick inserted into center comes out clean. Cool in pan 15 minutes; remove to wire rack to cool completely.

Orange-Lemon Citrus Bread

Makes 1 loaf

1¾ cups all-purpose flour

¾ cup sugar

1 tablespoon plus ½ teaspoon grated lemon peel, divided

2 teaspoons baking powder

1½ teaspoons grated orange peel

¼ teaspoon salt

1 cup milk

½ cup vegetable oil

1 egg, beaten

1 teaspoon vanilla

¼ cup orange marmalade

1. Preheat oven to 350°F. Grease and flour 9×5-inch loaf pan.

2. Combine flour, sugar, 1 tablespoon lemon peel, baking powder, orange peel and salt in large bowl; mix well.

3. Whisk milk, oil, egg and vanilla in small bowl until well blended. Add to flour mixture; stir just until blended. (Batter will be thin.) Pour batter into prepared pan.

4. Bake 45 minutes or until toothpick inserted into center comes out clean. Cool in pan 5 minutes.

5. Meanwhile, combine marmalade and remaining ½ teaspoon lemon peel in small microwavable bowl; microwave on HIGH 15 seconds or until slightly melted. Remove bread to wire rack; spread marmalade mixture evenly over top. Cool completely before serving.

Boston Black Coffee Bread

Makes 1 loaf

½ **cup rye flour**

½ **cup cornmeal**

½ **cup whole wheat flour**

1 **teaspoon baking soda**

½ **teaspoon salt**

¾ **cup strong brewed coffee, room temperature or cold**

⅓ **cup molasses**

¼ **cup vegetable oil**

¾ **cup raisins**

1. Preheat oven to 325°F. Grease and flour 9×5-inch loaf pan.

2. Combine rye flour, cornmeal, whole wheat flour, baking soda and salt in medium bowl; mix well. Add coffee, molasses and oil; stir until mixture forms thick batter. Stir in raisins. Spread batter in prepared pan.

3. Bake 50 minutes or until toothpick inserted into center comes out clean. Cool completely in pan on wire rack.

Tip: To cool hot coffee, pour over 2 ice cubes in a measuring cup to measure ¾ cup total. Let stand 10 minutes to cool.

Brown Soda Bread

Makes 6 to 8 servings

2 cups all-purpose flour

1 cup whole wheat flour

1 teaspoon baking soda

½ teaspoon salt

½ teaspoon ground ginger

1¼ to 1½ cups buttermilk

3 tablespoons dark molasses (preferably blackstrap)

1. Preheat oven to 375°F. Line baking sheet with parchment paper.

2. Combine 2 cups all-purpose flour, whole wheat flour, baking soda, salt and ginger in large bowl; mix well.

3. Whisk 1¼ cups buttermilk and molasses in small bowl until blended. Stir into flour mixture; add additional buttermilk, 1 tablespoon at a time, if needed to make dry, rough dough.

4. Turn out dough onto floured surface; knead 8 to 10 times or just until smooth. (Do not overknead.) Shape dough into round loaf about 1½ inches thick. Place on prepared baking sheet.

5. Use floured knife to cut halfway through dough, scoring into quarters. Sprinkle top of dough with additional all-purpose flour, if desired.

6. Bake about 35 minutes or until bread sounds hollow when tapped. Remove to wire rack to cool slightly. Serve warm.

Marbled Banana Bread

Makes 1 loaf

2 cups all-purpose flour	1½ cups mashed ripe bananas (about 3 medium)
1 teaspoon baking soda	2 eggs
1 teaspoon salt	½ cup sour cream
1 cup sugar	1 teaspoon vanilla
6 tablespoons (¾ stick) butter, softened	¾ cup semisweet chocolate chips

1. Preheat oven to 350°F. Spray 9×5-inch loaf pan with nonstick cooking spray or line with parchment paper.

2. Combine flour, baking soda and salt in medium bowl; mix well. Beat sugar and butter in large bowl with wooden spoon until well blended. Add bananas, eggs, sour cream and vanilla; stir until blended. Add flour mixture; stir just until dry ingredients are moistened.

3. Place chocolate chips in medium microwavable bowl; microwave on HIGH 1 minute. Stir until chocolate is melted and smooth; let cool 3 minutes. Add 1 cup batter to melted chocolate; stir until well blended.

4. Spoon plain and chocolate batters alternately into prepared pan; swirl batters together with knife or wooden skewer to marbleize.

5. Bake 1 hour to 1 hour and 5 minutes or until toothpick inserted into center comes out clean. Cool in pan 10 minutes; remove to wire rack to cool completely.

Date Nut Bread

Makes 1 loaf

2 cups all-purpose flour

½ cup packed brown sugar

1 tablespoon baking powder

½ teaspoon salt

¼ cup (½ stick) cold butter, cut into small pieces

1 cup chopped walnuts, toasted*

1 cup chopped dates

1¼ cups milk

1 egg

½ teaspoon grated lemon peel

*To toast walnuts, spread on ungreased baking sheet. Bake in preheated 350°F oven 6 to 8 minutes or until lightly browned, stirring occasionally.

1. Preheat oven to 375°F. Spray 9×5-inch loaf pan with nonstick cooking spray.

2. Combine flour, brown sugar, baking powder and salt in large bowl; mix well. Cut in butter with pastry blender or two knives until mixture resembles fine crumbs. Add walnuts and dates; stir until coated.

3. Whisk milk, egg and lemon peel in small bowl until blended. Add to flour mixture; stir just until moistened. Spread batter in prepared pan.

4. Bake 45 to 50 minutes or until toothpick inserted into center comes out clean. Cool in pan 10 minutes; remove to wire rack to cool completely.

Rhubarb Bread

Makes 1 loaf

2 cups all-purpose flour

1 cup sugar

1 tablespoon baking powder

1 teaspoon salt

¼ teaspoon ground cinnamon

1 cup milk

2 eggs

⅓ cup butter, melted

2 teaspoons grated fresh ginger (about 1 inch)

10 ounces chopped fresh rhubarb (¼-inch pieces, about 2¼ cups total)

¾ cup chopped walnuts, toasted*

*To toast walnuts, spread on ungreased baking sheet. Bake in preheated 350°F oven 6 to 8 minutes or until lightly browned, stirring occasionally.

1. Preheat oven to 350°F. Spray 9×5-inch loaf pan with nonstick cooking spray.

2. Combine flour, sugar, baking powder, salt and cinnamon in large bowl; mix well.

3. Whisk milk, eggs, butter and ginger in medium bowl until well blended. Add to flour mixture; stir just until dry ingredients are moistened. Add rhubarb and walnuts; stir just until blended. Pour batter into prepared pan.

4. Bake 60 to 65 minutes or until toothpick inserted into center comes out clean. Cool in pan 15 minutes; remove to wire rack to cool completely.

Pumpkin Bread

Makes 2 loaves

2¼ cups all-purpose flour

1 tablespoon pumpkin pie spice

1 teaspoon baking powder

1 teaspoon baking soda

¾ teaspoon salt

3 eggs

1 can (15 ounces) pure pumpkin

1 cup granulated sugar

1 cup packed brown sugar

⅔ cup vegetable oil

1 teaspoon vanilla

¼ cup roasted salted pumpkin seeds, coarsely chopped or crushed

1. Preheat oven to 350°F. Spray two 8×4-inch loaf pans with nonstick cooking spray.

2. Combine flour, pumpkin pie spice, baking powder, baking soda and salt in medium bowl; mix well.

3. Whisk eggs in large bowl. Add pumpkin, granulated sugar, brown sugar, oil and vanilla; whisk until well blended. Add flour mixture; stir just until dry ingredients are moistened. Divide batter between prepared pans; smooth tops. Sprinkle with pumpkin seeds; pat seeds gently into batter to adhere.

4. Bake about 50 minutes or until toothpick inserted into centers comes out mostly clean with just a few moist crumbs. Cool in pans 10 minutes; remove to wire racks to cool completely.

Note: The recipe can be made in one 9×5-inch loaf pan instead of two 8×4-inch pans. Bake about 1 hour 20 minutes or until toothpick inserted into center comes out with just a few moist crumbs. Check bread after 50 minutes; cover loosely with foil if top is browning too quickly.

Golden Corn Bread

Makes 9 to 12 servings

1¼ cups all-purpose flour

¾ cup yellow cornmeal

⅓ cup sugar

2 teaspoons baking powder

1 teaspoon salt

1¼ cups whole milk

¼ cup (½ stick) butter, melted

1 egg

Honey Butter (recipe follows, optional)

1. Preheat oven to 400°F. Spray 8-inch square baking dish or pan with nonstick cooking spray.

2. Combine flour, cornmeal, sugar, baking powder and salt in large bowl; mix well.

3. Whisk milk, butter and egg in medium bowl until well blended. Add to flour mixture; stir just until dry ingredients are moistened. Pour batter into prepared baking dish.

4. Bake 25 minutes or until golden brown and toothpick inserted into center comes out clean. Prepare Honey Butter, if desired. Serve with corn bread.

Honey Butter: Beat 6 tablespoons (¾ stick) softened butter and ¼ cup honey in medium bowl with electric mixer at medium-high speed until light and creamy.

Zucchini Bread

Makes 1 loaf

2 cups all-purpose flour

1 teaspoon salt

1 teaspoon ground cinnamon

¾ teaspoon baking powder

¾ teaspoon baking soda

¼ teaspoon ground nutmeg

½ cup vegetable oil

2 eggs

½ cup granulated sugar

½ cup packed brown sugar

1 teaspoon vanilla

2 cups packed grated zucchini (2 to 3 medium)

1. Preheat oven to 350°F. Spray 9×5-inch loaf pan with nonstick cooking spray or line with parchment paper.

2. Combine flour, salt, cinnamon, baking powder, baking soda and nutmeg in medium bowl; mix well.

3. Whisk oil, eggs, granulated sugar, brown sugar and vanilla in large bowl until well blended. Add flour mixture; stir just until dry ingredients are moistened. Stir in zucchini until blended. Spread batter in prepared pan.

4. Bake 55 to 60 minutes or until toothpick inserted into center comes out clean. Cool in pan 20 minutes; remove to wire rack to cool completely.

Keto Bread

Makes 1 loaf

7 **tablespoons butter, divided**	6 **eggs, at room temperature, separated***
2 **cups almond flour**	¼ **teaspoon cream of tartar**
3½ **teaspoons baking powder**	*Discard 1 egg yolk.*
½ **teaspoon salt**	

1. Preheat oven to 375°F. Generously grease 8×4-inch loaf pan with 1 tablespoon butter. Melt remaining 6 tablespoons butter; cool slightly.

2. Combine almond flour, baking powder and salt in medium bowl; mix well. Add melted butter and 5 egg yolks; stir until blended.

3. Combine egg whites and cream of tartar in large bowl of stand mixer. Use whip attachment to beat egg whites at high speed 1 to 2 minutes or until stiff peaks form.

4. Stir one third of egg whites into almond flour mixture until well blended (batter will be very stiff). Gently fold in remaining egg whites until thoroughly blended (batter may look mottled). Scrape batter into prepared pan; smooth top.

5. Bake 25 to 30 minutes or until top is light brown and dry and toothpick inserted into center comes out clean. Cool in pan 10 minutes; remove to wire rack to cool completely.

Loaded Banana Bread

Makes 1 loaf

1½ cups all-purpose flour
2½ teaspoons baking powder
¼ teaspoon salt
6 tablespoons (¾ stick) butter, softened
⅓ cup granulated sugar
⅓ cup packed brown sugar
2 eggs

3 ripe bananas, mashed
½ teaspoon vanilla
1 can (8 ounces) crushed pineapple, drained
⅓ cup flaked coconut
¼ cup mini chocolate chips
⅓ cup chopped walnuts (optional)

1. Preheat oven to 350°F. Spray 9×5-inch loaf pan with nonstick cooking spray.

2. Sift flour, baking powder and salt into small bowl. Beat butter, granulated sugar and brown sugar in large bowl with electric mixer at medium speed until light and fluffy. Beat in eggs, one at a time, scraping down bowl after each addition. Add bananas and vanilla; beat at low speed just until blended.

3. Slowly add flour mixture; beat just until combined. Fold in pineapple, coconut and chocolate chips. Spread batter in prepared pan; top with walnuts, if desired.

4. Bake 50 minutes or until toothpick inserted into center comes out almost clean. Cool in pan 1 hour; remove to wire rack to cool completely.

Muffins

Raspberry Corn Muffins

Makes 12 muffins

1 cup all-purpose flour

¾ cup yellow cornmeal

½ cup sugar

2 teaspoons baking powder

½ teaspoon baking soda

¼ teaspoon salt

⅔ cup Greek yogurt or sour cream

⅓ cup milk

¼ cup (½ stick) butter, melted

1 egg

1¼ cups fresh or frozen raspberries

1. Preheat oven to 350°F. Spray 12 standard (2½-inch) muffin cups with nonstick cooking spray.

2. Combine flour, cornmeal, sugar, baking powder, baking soda and salt in large bowl; mix well.

3. Whisk yogurt, milk, butter and egg in medium bowl until well blended. Add to flour mixture; stir just until dry ingredients are moistened. Gently fold in raspberries. Spoon batter into prepared muffin cups, filling three-fourths full.

4. Bake 18 to 20 minutes or until golden brown. Cool in pan 5 minutes; remove to wire rack to cool slightly.

Baby Bran Muffins

Makes 24 muffins

1 cup whole bran cereal

1 cup milk

1 egg, beaten

2 tablespoons butter, melted

1 cup all-purpose flour

¼ cup packed brown sugar

2½ teaspoons baking powder

½ teaspoon baking soda

¼ teaspoon salt

¼ teaspoon ground cinnamon

¼ cup currants

Orange Cream Cheese Spread (optional, recipe follows)

1. Preheat oven to 375°F. Spray 24 mini (1¾-inch) muffin cups with nonstick cooking spray.

2. Combine cereal, milk, egg and butter in large bowl; let stand 10 minutes.

3. Combine flour, brown sugar, baking powder, baking soda, salt and cinnamon in medium bowl; mix well. Add to cereal mixture; stir just until blended. Fold in currants. Spoon batter into prepared muffin cups, filling three-fourths full.

4. Bake 15 minutes or until firm when lightly pressed. Cool in pans 1 minute; remove to wire racks to cool completely. Prepare cream cheese spread, if desired; serve with muffins.

Orange Cream Cheese Spread: Beat 1 package (8 ounces) softened cream cheese, 3 tablespooons orange juice and 1 teaspoon granulated sugar in medium bowl with electric mixer at high speed 1 minute or until light and fluffy.

Mixed-Up Muffins

Makes 15 muffins

2 cups all-purpose flour

1 cup sugar, divided

2 teaspoons baking powder

½ teaspoon baking soda

¼ teaspoon salt

⅓ cup mini chocolate chips

⅓ cup unsweetened cocoa powder

1¼ cups milk

2 eggs

⅓ cup vegetable oil

1 teaspoon vanilla

1. Preheat oven to 400°F. Line 15 standard (2½-inch) muffin cups with paper baking cups or spray with nonstick cooking spray.

2. Combine flour, ¾ cup sugar, baking powder, baking soda and salt in medium bowl; mix well. Remove 1½ cups mixture to separate bowl; stir in chocolate chips. Stir cocoa and remaining ¼ cup sugar into remaining flour mixture.

3. Whisk milk, eggs, oil and vanilla in small bowl until blended. Add half of milk mixture to each bowl of dry ingredients; stir each batter separately just until dry ingredients are moistened. Spoon white and chocolate batters side by side into prepared muffin cups, filling about three-fourths full.

4. Bake 20 to 25 minutes or until toothpick inserted into centers comes out clean. Cool in pans 2 minutes; remove to wire racks. Serve warm or at room temperature.

Sweet Potato Muffins

Makes 12 muffins

⅓ cup plus 2 tablespoons packed brown sugar, divided

2 teaspoons ground cinnamon, divided

1½ cups all-purpose flour

2 teaspoons baking powder

½ teaspoon baking soda

½ teaspoon salt

½ teaspoon ground allspice

1 cup mashed cooked or canned sweet potatoes

¾ cup buttermilk

¼ cup vegetable oil

1 egg

1. Preheat oven to 425°F. Spray 12 standard (2½-inch) muffin cups with nonstick cooking spray.

2. Combine 2 tablespoons brown sugar and 1 teaspoon cinnamon in small bowl; mix well. Combine flour, remaining ⅓ cup brown sugar, 1 teaspoon cinnamon, baking powder, baking soda, salt and allspice in large bowl; mix well.

3. Whisk sweet potatoes, buttermilk, oil and egg in medium bowl until well blended. Add to flour mixture; stir just until dry ingredients are moistened. Spoon evenly into prepared muffin cups; sprinkle with brown sugar-cinnamon mixture.

4. Bake 14 to 16 minutes or until toothpick inserted into centers comes out clean. Remove to wire rack to cool completely.

Sun-Dried Tomato Basil Muffins

Makes 12 muffins

½ **cups sun-dried tomatoes (about 12 pieces, not oil-packed)**

2 **cups all-purpose flour**

1 **tablespoon baking powder**

1½ **teaspoons dried basil**

½ **teaspoon salt**

¼ **teaspoon black pepper**

⅛ **teaspoon garlic powder**

¾ **cup milk**

½ **cup cottage cheese**

1 **egg**

¼ **cup vegetable or canola oil**

2 **teaspoons minced dried onion**

1. Preheat oven to 400°F. Spray 12 standard (2½-inch) muffin cups with nonstick cooking spray or line with foil or paper baking cups.

2. Cover sun-dried tomatoes with hot water in small bowl; let stand 10 minutes to soften. Drain and finely chop.

3. Combine flour, baking powder, basil, salt, pepper and garlic powder in large bowl; mix well. Whisk milk, cottage cheese, egg, oil, onion and sun-dried tomatoes in separate medium bowl until well blended. Add to flour mixture; stir just until dry ingredients are moistened. Spoon batter evenly into prepared muffin cups.

4. Bake 20 to 25 minutes or until toothpick inserted into centers comes out clean. Cool in pan 5 minutes. Serve warm.

Banana Walnut Muffins

Makes 12 muffins

2 cups all-purpose flour

2 teaspoons baking powder

½ teaspoon baking soda

½ teaspoon ground cinnamon

¼ teaspoon salt

¼ teaspoon ground nutmeg

½ cup (1 stick) butter, softened

1 cup packed brown sugar

2 eggs, lightly beaten

1 teaspoon vanilla

3 ripe bananas

¼ cup sour cream

1 cup coarsely chopped walnuts, toasted*

*To toast walnuts, spread on baking sheet. Bake in preheated 350°F oven 6 to 8 minutes or until lightly browned, stirring occasionally.

1. Preheat oven to 375°F. Line 12 standard (2½-inch) muffin cups with paper baking cups or spray with nonstick cooking spray.

2. Combine flour, baking powder, baking soda, cinnamon, salt and nutmeg in small bowl; mix well.

3. Beat butter in large bowl with electric mixer at medium speed 2 minutes or until light and fluffy. Add brown sugar; beat until well blended. Add eggs and vanilla; beat until blended. Mash bananas in medium bowl. Stir in sour cream until blended. Add to butter mixture; beat until smooth.

4. Slowly add flour mixture, stirring just until blended. Stir in walnuts. Spoon batter evenly into prepared muffin cups.

5. Bake 25 minutes or until toothpick inserted into centers comes out clean. Cool in pan 10 minutes; remove to wire rack to cool completely.

Cherry Lemon Poppy Seed Muffins

Makes 12 muffins

2 cups all-purpose flour

1 cup sugar

1 tablespoon baking powder

1 teaspoon salt

¾ cup buttermilk

¼ cup vegetable oil

¼ cup (½ stick) butter, melted

2 eggs

Grated peel of 1 lemon

1 tablespoon fresh lemon juice

1 teaspoon vanilla

½ cup dried sweet cherries, chopped

½ cup chopped pecans

2 tablespoons poppy seeds

1. Preheat oven to 350°F. Spray 12 standard (2½-inch) muffin cups with nonstick cooking spray or line with paper baking cups.

2. Combine flour, sugar, baking powder and salt in large bowl; mix well.

3. Whisk buttermilk, oil, butter, eggs, lemon peel, lemon juice and vanilla in medium bowl until well blended. Add to flour mixture; stir just until dry ingredients are moistened. Stir in cherries, pecans and poppy seeds just until blended. Spoon batter evenly into prepared muffin cups.

4. Bake 20 to 24 minutes or until golden brown and toothpick inserted into centers comes out clean. Cool in pan 5 minutes; remove to wire rack to cool completely.

Apple Date Nut Muffins

Makes 12 muffins

1½ cups all-purpose flour

⅔ cup packed brown sugar

½ cup old-fashioned oats

1 tablespoon baking powder

1 teaspoon ground cinnamon

½ teaspoon salt

⅛ teaspoon ground nutmeg

⅛ teaspoon ground ginger

Pinch ground cloves

1 cup coarsely chopped peeled apples

½ cup chopped walnuts

½ cup chopped pitted dates

½ cup (1 stick) butter, melted

2 eggs

¼ cup milk

1. Preheat oven to 400°F. Line 12 standard (2½-inch) muffin cups with paper baking cups or spray with nonstick cooking spray.

2. Combine flour, brown sugar, oats, baking powder, cinnamon, salt, nutmeg, ginger and cloves in large bowl; mix well. Stir in apples, walnuts and dates.

3. Whisk butter, eggs and milk in small bowl until blended. Add to flour mixture; stir just until dry ingredients are moistened. Spoon batter evenly into prepared muffin cups.

4. Bake 20 to 25 minutes or until toothpick inserted into centers comes out clean. Remove to wire rack to cool completely.

Lemon-Glazed
Zucchini Muffins

Makes 12 muffins

2 cups all-purpose flour

⅔ cup granulated sugar

1 tablespoon baking powder

1 teaspoon salt

½ teaspoon ground nutmeg

2 teaspoons grated lemon peel

½ cup chopped walnuts, pecans or hazelnuts

½ cup dried fruit bits or golden raisins

½ cup milk

⅓ cup vegetable oil

2 eggs

1 cup packed shredded zucchini

1½ teaspoons lemon juice

¼ cup powdered sugar

1. Preheat oven to 400°F. Spray 12 standard (2½-inch) muffin cups with nonstick cooking spray or line with paper baking cups.

2. Combine flour, granulated sugar, baking powder, salt, nutmeg and lemon peel in large bowl; mix well. Stir in walnuts and fruit.

3. Whisk milk, oil and eggs in small bowl until blended. Add to flour mixture with zucchini; stir just until dry ingredients are moistened. Spoon batter evenly into prepared muffin cups.

4. Bake 20 to 25 minutes or until toothpick inserted into centers comes out clean. Remove to wire rack.

5. Meanwhile, stir lemon juice into powdered sugar in small bowl until smooth. Drizzle glaze over warm muffins.

Cinnamon-Sugared Pumpkin Pecan Muffins

Makes 12 servings

8 tablespoons sugar, divided

2 teaspoons ground cinnamon, divided

1 cup 100% bran cereal

1 cup milk

1 cup all-purpose flour

1 tablespoon baking powder

½ teaspoon baking soda

½ teaspoon salt

1 cup canned pumpkin

1 egg, beaten

1 tablespoon vanilla

1 package (2 ounces) pecan chips (½ cup)

1. Preheat oven to 400°F. Spray 12 standard (2½-inch) nonstick muffin cups with nonstick cooking spray.

2. Combine 2 tablespoons sugar and ½ teaspoon cinnamon in small bowl; mix well. Combine cereal and milk in large bowl; let stand 5 minutes to soften.

3. Combine flour, remaining 6 tablespoons sugar, 1½ teaspoons cinnamon, baking powder, baking soda and salt in large bowl; mix well.

4. Whisk pumpkin, egg and vanilla into cereal mixture until well blended. Add flour mixture; stir just until dry ingredients are moistened. Spoon batter evenly into prepared muffin cups; sprinkle with pecan chips and cinnamon-sugar.

5. Bake 20 to 25 minutes or until toothpick inserted into centers comes out clean. Cool in pan 3 minutes; remove to wire rack. Serve warm or at room temperature.

Maple Magic Muffins

Makes 12 muffins

½ cup plus 3 tablespoons pure maple syrup, divided

¼ cup chopped walnuts

2 tablespoons butter, melted

2 cups all-purpose flour

¾ cup sugar

2 teaspoons baking powder

½ teaspoon baking soda

½ teaspoon salt

¼ teaspoon ground cinnamon

¾ cup plus 1 tablespoon milk

½ cup vegetable oil

1 egg

½ teaspoon vanilla

1. Preheat oven to 400°F. Spray 12 standard (2½-inch) muffin cups with nonstick cooking spray.

2. Pour 2 teaspoons maple syrup into each muffin cup; top with 1 teaspoon walnuts and ½ teaspoon butter.

3. Combine flour, sugar, baking powder, baking soda, salt and cinnamon in large bowl; mix well.

4. Whisk milk, oil, egg, remaining 3 tablespoons maple syrup and vanilla in medium bowl until well blended. Add to flour mixture; stir just until dry ingredients are moistened. Spoon batter into prepared muffin cups, filling two-thirds full. Place muffin pan on baking sheet to catch any drips (maple syrup may overflow slightly).

5. Bake 20 to 25 minutes or until toothpick inserted into centers comes out clean. Invert pan onto wire rack covered with waxed paper. Cool in pan 5 minutes; serve warm.

Jalapeño Corn Muffins

Makes 18 muffins

1½ cups yellow cornmeal

¾ cup all-purpose flour

2 teaspoons baking powder

½ teaspoon baking soda

½ teaspoon salt

2 eggs

4 tablespoons (½ stick) butter, melted and cooled

2 tablespoons sugar

¾ cup buttermilk

1 can (8 ounces) cream-style corn

1 cup (4 ounces) Monterey Jack or Cheddar cheese

2 jalapeño peppers,* seeded and finely chopped

*Jalapeño peppers can sting and irritate the skin, so wear rubber gloves when handling peppers and do not touch your eyes.

1. Preheat oven to 400°F. Spray 18 standard (2½-inch) muffin cups with nonstick cooking spray or line with paper baking cups.

2. Combine cornmeal, flour, baking powder, baking soda and salt in large bowl; mix well.

3. Beat eggs in medium bowl; stir in butter and sugar until blended. Stir in buttermilk. Add to flour mixture; stir just until blended. Add corn, cheese and jalapeños; stir gently just until blended. Spoon batter into prepared muffin cups, filling three-fourths full.

4. Bake 15 to 17 minutes or until golden brown. Cool in pans 5 minutes; serve warm.

Classic Blueberry Muffins

Makes 15 muffins

1½ **cups fresh or frozen blueberries (do not thaw)**

2 **cups all-purpose flour, divided**

¾ **cup sugar**

2 **teaspoons baking powder**

½ **teaspoon baking soda**

½ **teaspoon ground cinnamon**

¼ **teaspoon salt**

Pinch ground nutmeg

¾ **cup plus 2 tablespoons milk**

½ **cup (1 stick) butter, melted**

1 **egg**

1 **teaspoon vanilla**

1. Preheat oven to 400°F. Line 15 standard (2½-inch) muffin cups with paper baking cups or spray with nonstick cooking spray.

2. Combine blueberries and 2 tablespoons flour in small bowl; toss gently to coat.

3. Combine remaining flour, sugar, baking powder, baking soda, cinnamon, salt and nutmeg in large bowl; mix well.

4. Whisk milk, butter, egg and vanilla in medium bowl until well blended. Add to flour mixture; stir just until dry ingredients are moistened. Gently fold in blueberries. Spoon batter into prepared muffin cups, filling three-fourths full.

5. Bake 20 to 25 minutes or until toothpick inserted into centers comes out clean. Cool in pans 2 minutes; remove to wire racks. Serve warm or at room temperature.

Biscuits

Ham and Swiss Cheese Biscuits

Makes about 18 biscuits

2 cups all-purpose flour

2 teaspoons baking powder

½ teaspoon baking soda

½ cup (1 stick) cold butter, cut into small pieces

⅔ cup buttermilk

½ cup (2 ounces) shredded Swiss cheese

2 ounces ham, minced

1. Preheat oven to 450°F. Line baking sheet with parchment paper or spray with nonstick cooking spray.

2. Combine flour, baking powder and baking soda in medium bowl; mix well. Cut in butter with pastry blender or two knives until mixture resembles coarse crumbs.

3. Stir in buttermilk, 1 tablespoon at a time, until slightly sticky dough forms. Stir in cheese and ham.

4. Turn out dough onto lightly floured surface; knead lightly. Roll out dough to ½-inch thickness. Cut out biscuits with 2-inch round cutter. Place on prepared baking sheet.

5. Bake 10 minutes or until browned. Serve warm.

Sweet Potato Biscuits

Makes about 12 biscuits

2½ cups all-purpose flour

¼ cup packed brown sugar

1 tablespoon baking powder

¾ teaspoon salt

¾ teaspoon ground cinnamon

¼ teaspoon ground ginger

¼ teaspoon ground allspice

½ cup cold shortening, cut into small pieces

½ cup chopped pecans

¾ cup mashed canned sweet potatoes

½ cup milk

1. Preheat oven to 450°F.

2. Combine flour, brown sugar, baking powder, salt, cinnamon, ginger and allspice in medium bowl; mix well. Cut in shortening with pastry blender or two knives until mixture resembles coarse crumbs. Stir in pecans.

3. Whisk sweet potatoes and milk in small bowl until smooth. Add to flour mixture; stir until soft dough forms.

4. Turn out dough onto lightly floured surface; knead lightly. Roll out dough to ½-inch thickness. Cut out biscuits with 2½-inch round cutter. Place on ungreased baking sheet.

5. Bake 12 to 14 minutes or until golden brown. Serve warm.

Country Buttermilk Biscuits

Makes about 9 biscuits

2 cups all-purpose flour

1 tablespoon baking powder

2 teaspoons sugar

½ teaspoon salt

½ teaspoon baking soda

⅓ cup cold shortening, cut into small pieces

⅔ cup buttermilk*

*Or substitute 2½ teaspoons lemon juice plus enough milk to equal ⅔ cup. Stir; let stand 5 minutes before using.

1. Preheat oven to 450°F.

2. Combine flour, baking powder, sugar, salt and baking soda in medium bowl; mix well. Cut in shortening with pastry blender or two knives until mixture resembles coarse crumbs.

3. Stir in buttermilk until soft dough forms that clings together and forms a ball.

4. Turn out dough onto well-floured surface; knead gently 10 to 12 times. Roll or pat dough to ½-inch thickness. Cut out biscuits with floured 2½-inch round cutter. Place 2 inches apart on ungreased baking sheet.

5. Bake 8 to 10 minutes or until golden brown. Serve warm.

Sour Cream Dill Biscuits: Prepare Country Buttermilk Biscuits as directed in step 2. Omit buttermilk; combine ½ cup sour cream, ⅓ cup milk and 1 tablespoon chopped fresh dill *or* 1 teaspoon dried dill weed in small bowl until well blended. Stir into flour-shortening mixture. Continue as directed.

Bacon and Onion Biscuits: Prepare Country Buttermilk Biscuits as directed in step 2, adding 4 slices crumbled crisp-cooked bacon and ⅓ cup chopped green onions to flour-shortening mixture before adding buttermilk. Continue as directed.

Wheaty Cranberry Biscuits

Makes 8 biscuits

1 cup all-purpose flour

1 cup whole wheat flour

3 tablespoons sugar

2½ teaspoons baking powder

½ teaspoon salt

½ teaspoon baking soda

½ cup (1 stick) cold butter, cut into small pieces

¾ cup buttermilk

½ cup dried cranberries

⅓ cup all-bran cereal

1. Preheat oven to 425°F. Line baking sheet with parchment paper or spray with nonstick cooking spray.

2. Combine all-purpose flour, whole wheat flour, sugar, baking powder, salt and baking soda in large bowl; mix well. Cut in butter with pastry blender or two knives until mixture resembles coarse crumbs.

3. Stir in buttermilk until soft, slightly sticky dough forms. Stir in cranberries and cereal.

4. Turn out dough onto lightly floured surface. Pat or roll out dough to ¾-inch thickness. Cut out biscuits with 2½-inch round cutter. Place on prepared baking sheet.

5. Bake 15 minutes or until golden brown. Serve warm.

Mustard-Pepper Biscuits

Makes 14 biscuits

2 cups all-purpose flour

1 tablespoon baking powder

1 teaspoon sugar

¾ teaspoon black pepper

½ teaspoon salt

⅛ teaspoon garlic powder

3 tablespoons cold butter, cut into small pieces

¾ cup milk

2 tablespoons Dijon mustard

1. Preheat oven to 450°F. Line baking sheet with parchment paper or spray with nonstick cooking spray.

2. Combine flour, baking powder, sugar, pepper, salt and garlic powder in medium bowl; mix well. Cut in butter with pastry blender or two knives until mixture resembles coarse crumbs.

3. Whisk milk and mustard in small bowl until blended. Add to flour mixture; stir just until dry ingredients are moistened. Drop dough by rounded tablespoonfuls 1 inch apart on prepared baking sheet.

4. Bake about 10 minutes or until golden brown. Serve warm.

Oatmeal Drop Biscuits

Makes about 16 biscuits

1½ cups all-purpose flour

½ cup quick oats

1 tablespoon baking powder

2 teaspoons sugar

½ teaspoon salt

½ teaspoon grated orange peel

6 tablespoons (¾ stick) cold butter, cut into small pieces

¾ cup milk

1. Preheat oven to 450°F.

2. Combine flour, oats, baking powder, sugar, salt and orange peel in large bowl; mix well. Cut in butter with pastry blender or two knives until mixture resembles coarse crumbs.

3. Slowly stir in ¼ cup milk, then continue adding milk, 1 tablespoon at a time, until slightly sticky dough forms. Drop dough by rounded tablespoonfuls 2 inches apart onto ungreased baking sheets.

4. Bake 10 to 12 minutes until bottoms are golden brown. Serve warm.

Peanut Butter and Jelly Monkey Biscuits

Makes 12 servings

¼ cup creamy peanut butter

2 tablespoons butter

2¼ cups all-purpose flour

¼ cup sugar

1 tablespoon baking powder

½ teaspoon salt

¼ cup (½ stick) cold butter, cut into small pieces

¾ cup buttermilk

6 tablespoons seedless strawberry jam, or favorite flavor

1. Preheat oven to 350°F. Line 9×5-inch loaf pan with foil, leaving 2-inch overhang. Spray foil with nonstick cooking spray.

2. Combine peanut butter and 2 tablespoons butter in small saucepan; cook and stir over low heat until melted. Cool slightly.

3. Combine flour, sugar, baking powder and salt in medium bowl; mix well. Cut in ¼ cup cold butter with pastry blender or two knives until mixture resembles coarse crumbs. Stir in buttermilk just until moistened.

4. Turn out dough onto lightly floured surface; knead six to eight times. Pat dough into 8×6-inch rectangle; cut into 1-inch squares. Roll one third of squares in peanut butter mixture to coat; place in single layer in prepared pan. Top with 2 tablespoons jam (drop jam by spoonfuls evenly over squares). Repeat layers twice.

5. Bake 35 to 40 minutes or until jam is melted and bubbly and biscuits are flaky. Cool in pan on wire rack 10 minutes. Remove biscuits from pan using foil. Serve warm.

Green Onion Cream Cheese Biscuits

Makes 8 biscuits

2 cups all-purpose flour

1 tablespoon baking powder

1 tablespoon sugar

¾ teaspoon salt

3 ounces cream cheese

¼ cup cold shortening, cut into small pieces

½ cup finely chopped green onions

⅔ cup milk

1. Preheat oven to 450°F.

2. Combine flour, baking powder, sugar and salt in medium bowl; mix well. Cut in cream cheese and shortening with pastry blender or two knives until mixture resembles coarse crumbs. Stir in green onions.

3. Stir in milk until soft dough forms that clings together and forms a ball.

4. Turn out dough onto well-floured surface; knead gently 10 to 12 times. Roll or pat dough to ½-inch thickness. Cut out biscuits with floured 3-inch round cutter. Place 2 inches apart on ungreased baking sheet.

5. Bake 10 to 12 minutes or until golden brown. Serve warm.

Sweet Cherry Biscuits

Makes about 10 biscuits

2 cups all-purpose flour

2 tablespoons sugar

4 teaspoons baking powder

½ teaspoon salt

½ teaspoon dried rosemary, crushed (optional)

½ cup (1 stick) cold butter, cut into small pieces

¾ cup milk

½ cup dried sweetened cherries, chopped

1. Preheat oven to 425°F.

2. Combine flour, sugar, baking powder, salt and rosemary, if desired, in large bowl; mix well. Cut in butter with pastry blender or two knives until mixture forms coarse crumbs.

3. Stir in milk until sticky dough forms. Fold in cherries.

4. Turn out dough onto lightly floured surface. Pat dough to 1-inch thickness. Cut out biscuits with 3-inch round cutter. Place 1 inch apart on ungreased baking sheet.

5. Bake 15 minutes or until golden brown. Cool on wire rack 5 minutes before serving.

Cheddar Biscuits

Makes 15 biscuits

2 cups all-purpose flour

1 tablespoon sugar

1 tablespoon baking powder

2¼ teaspoons garlic powder, divided

¾ teaspoon plus pinch of salt, divided

1 cup whole milk

½ cup (1 stick) plus 3 tablespoons butter, melted, divided

2 cups (8 ounces) shredded Cheddar cheese

½ teaspoon dried parsley flakes

1. Preheat oven to 450°F. Line baking sheet with parchment paper.

2. Combine flour, sugar, baking powder, 2 teaspoons garlic powder and ¾ teaspoon salt in large bowl; mix well.

3. Add milk and ½ cup butter; stir just until dry ingredients are moistened. Stir in cheese just until blended. Drop scant ¼ cupfuls of dough about 1½ inches apart onto prepared baking sheet.

4. Bake 10 to 12 minutes or until golden brown.

5. Meanwhile, combine remaining 3 tablespoons butter, ¼ teaspoon garlic powder, pinch of salt and parsley flakes in small bowl; brush over biscuits immediately after removing from oven. Serve warm.

Scones

Broccoli and Cheddar Scones

Makes 16 scones

2½ cups all-purpose flour

1 tablespoon baking powder

1 tablespoon sugar

2 teaspoons salt

½ teaspoon red pepper flakes

1 cup broccoli florets

½ cup (1 stick) cold butter, cut into small pieces

1½ cups (6 ounces) shredded Cheddar cheese

1 cup milk

1. Preheat oven to 400°F. Line two baking sheets with parchment paper.

2. Combine flour, baking powder, sugar, salt and red pepper flakes in food processor; process 10 seconds. Add broccoli and butter; process until mixture forms coarse meal, scraping down side of bowl once. Transfer mixture to large bowl.

3. Add cheese and milk; stir until blended. Knead gently to form dough.

4. Divide dough in half. Press one half of dough into 8-inch circle. Cut into eight wedges; place on prepared baking sheet. Repeat with remaining half of dough.

5. Bake 15 to 20 minutes or until lightly browned.

Orange Currant Scones

Makes 8 scones

1½ cups all-purpose flour

¼ cup plus 1 teaspoon sugar, divided

1 teaspoon baking powder

¼ teaspoon salt

¼ teaspoon baking soda

⅓ cup currants

1 tablespoon grated orange peel

6 tablespoons (¾ stick) cold butter, cut into small pieces

½ cup buttermilk, yogurt or sour cream

1. Preheat oven to 425°F. Line baking sheet with parchment paper or spray with nonstick cooking spray.

2. Combine flour, ¼ cup sugar, baking powder, salt and baking soda in large bowl. Stir in currants and orange peel. Cut in butter with pastry blender or two knives until mixture resembles coarse crumbs.

3. Slowly add buttermilk; stir to form soft, sticky dough that clings together.

4. Shape dough into a ball; pat into 8-inch round on prepared baking sheet. Cut dough into eight wedges with floured knife. Sprinkle with remaining 1 teaspoon sugar.

5. Bake 18 to 20 minutes or until lightly browned.

Cornmeal, Sunflower and Cranberry Scones

Makes 14 to 18 scones

1½ cups all-purpose flour

¾ cup salted roasted
    sunflower kernels

¾ cup sweetened dried
    cranberries

½ cup sugar

⅓ cup yellow cornmeal

3 tablespoons corn grits
    (polenta)

1 tablespoon baking
    powder

¼ teaspoon salt

½ cup (1 stick) cold butter,
    cut into small pieces

⅔ to ¾ cup half-and-half
    or milk

1. Preheat oven to 425°F. Line large baking sheet with parchment paper.

2. Combine flour, sunflower kernels, cranberries, sugar, cornmeal, corn grits, baking powder and salt in large bowl; mix well. Cut in butter with pastry blender or two knives until mixture resembles coarse crumbs.

3. Add half-and-half by ⅓ cupfuls; stir gently until dough comes together. (If dough is too dry, add additional half-and-half, 1 tablespoon at a time.) Drop dough by ¼ cupfuls 1 inch apart onto prepared baking sheet.

4. Bake 15 to 17 minutes or until golden brown. Cool on baking sheet 5 minutes; remove to wire rack.

Honey Scones

Makes 8 scones

2 cups all-purpose flour

½ cup old-fashioned oats

2 tablespoons packed
   brown sugar

1 tablespoon granulated
   sugar

1 tablespoon baking
   powder

½ teaspoon salt

6 tablespoons (¾ stick)
   butter, melted

1 egg

¼ cup whipping cream

¼ cup milk

3 tablespoons honey

1. Preheat oven to 425°F. Line baking sheet with parchment paper.

2. Combine flour, oats, brown sugar, granulated sugar, baking powder and salt in large bowl; mix well.

3. Whisk butter, egg, cream, milk and honey in medium bowl until well blended. Add to flour mixture; stir just until dough forms.

4. Turn out dough onto lightly floured surface; pat into 8-inch round about ¾ inch thick. Cut into eight wedges; place 1 to 2 inches apart on prepared baking sheet.

5. Bake 12 to 15 minutes or until golden brown. Cool on wire rack 15 minutes.

Raisin Oat Scones

Makes 30 scones

2 cups all-purpose flour

2 teaspoons baking powder

½ teaspoon baking soda

¼ teaspoon salt

1 cup old-fashioned oats

½ cup (1 stick) cold butter, cut into small pieces

1 cup raisins

1 cup buttermilk

1. Preheat oven to 425°F. Line baking sheet with parchment paper or spray with nonstick cooking spray.

2. Sift flour, baking powder, baking soda and salt into medium bowl. Stir in oats. Cut in butter with pastry blender or two knives until mixture resembles coarse crumbs. Stir in raisins.

3. Slowly add buttermilk; stir to form soft dough.

4. Turn out dough onto lightly floured surface; knead several times until smooth. Pat dough into 12×10-inch rectangle; cut into 2-inch squares. Place on prepared baking sheet.

5. Bake about 15 minutes or until golden brown.

Walnut Ginger Scones

Makes 8 scones

1 cup all-purpose flour

1 cup whole wheat flour

1 cup coarsely chopped walnuts, toasted*

¾ cup diced crystallized ginger

½ cup raisins

¼ cup plus 1 teaspoon sugar, divided

1 tablespoon baking powder

½ teaspoon salt

½ teaspoon ground cinnamon

½ cup (1 stick) cold butter, cut into small pieces

¾ to 1 cup half-and-half

*To toast walnuts, spread on ungreased baking sheet. Bake in preheated 350°F oven 6 to 8 minutes or until golden brown, stirring occasionally.

1. Preheat oven to 425°F. Line baking sheet with parchment paper or spray with nonstick cooking spray.

2. Combine all-purpose flour, whole wheat flour, walnuts, ginger, raisins, ¼ cup sugar, baking powder, salt and cinnamon in large bowl; mix well. Cut in butter with pastry blender or two knives until mixture is crumbly.

3. Add half-and-half by ¼ cupfuls; stir gently until dough comes together. Pat dough into 10-inch round on prepared baking sheet; sprinkle with remaining 1 teaspoon sugar. Cut into 10 wedges. Pull wedges apart, leaving 1 inch space between wedges.

4. Bake 15 minutes or until golden brown. Cool on baking sheet 10 minutes; remove to wire rack to cool completely.

Cinnamon Date Scones

Makes 12 scones

4 tablespoons sugar, divided

¼ teaspoon ground cinnamon

2 cups all-purpose flour

2½ teaspoons baking powder

½ teaspoon salt

5 tablespoons cold butter, cut into small pieces

½ cup chopped pitted dates

2 eggs

⅓ cup half-and-half or milk

1. Preheat oven to 425°F. Combine 2 tablespoons sugar and cinnamon in small bowl; mix well.

2. Combine flour, remaining 2 tablespoons sugar, baking powder and salt in medium bowl; mix well. Cut in butter with pastry blender or two knives until mixture resembles coarse crumbs. Stir in dates.

3. Beat eggs in separate small bowl. Add half-and-half; whisk until well blended. Reserve 1 tablespoon egg mixture for brushing scones. Add remaining egg mixture to flour mixture; stir to form soft dough that clings together and forms a ball.

4. Turn out dough onto well-floured surface; knead gently 10 to 12 times. Roll out dough into 9×6-inch rectangle. Cut into six 3-inch squares; cut each square diagonally in half. Place triangles 2 inches apart on ungreased baking sheets. Brush with reserved egg mixture; sprinkle with cinnamon-sugar.

5. Bake 10 to 12 minutes or until golden brown. Remove to wire racks to cool 10 minutes. Serve warm.

Berry Buckwheat Scones

Makes 8 scones

1¼ cups all-purpose flour

¾ cup buckwheat flour

¼ cup packed brown sugar

1 tablespoon baking powder

½ teaspoon salt

½ cup (1 stick) cold butter, cut into small pieces

¾ cup fresh raspberries

¾ cup fresh blackberries

1 egg

½ cup whipping cream

1 tablespoon granulated sugar

1. Preheat oven to 375°F. Line baking sheet with parchment paper.

2. Combine all-purpose flour, buckwheat flour, brown sugar, baking powder and salt in food processor; pulse until combined. Add butter; pulse until pea-sized pieces of butter remain. Transfer to large bowl; gently stir in berries.

3. Whisk egg and cream in small bowl until blended. Add to flour mixture; stir to form soft dough.

4. Turn out dough onto surface lightly dusted with buckwheat flour. Gently pat dough into 8-inch round about ¾ inch thick. Cut into eight wedges. Place wedges 1½ inches apart on prepared baking sheet; sprinkle with granulated sugar.

5. Bake 20 to 25 minutes or until golden brown. Remove to wire rack to cool 10 minutes. Serve warm.

Oat Pecan Scones

Makes 12 scones

1½ cups all-purpose flour

1 cup chopped pecans, toasted*

¾ cup old-fashioned oats, toasted**

½ cup raisins or currants

½ cup packed brown sugar

2½ teaspoons baking powder

1 teaspoon ground cinnamon

½ teaspoon baking soda

¼ teaspoon ground ginger

¼ teaspoon salt

½ cup (1 stick) cold butter, cut into small pieces

⅔ to ¾ cup half-and-half or milk

2 teaspoons granulated sugar

To toast pecans, spread on ungreased baking sheet. Bake in preheated 350°F oven 6 to 8 minutes or until golden brown, stirring occasionally.

**To toast oats, cook in large skillet over medium heat 1 to 2 minutes or until oats just begin to turn golden, stirring frequently. Remove from skillet immediately; cool before using.*

1. Preheat oven to 425°F. Line baking sheet with parchment paper or spray with nonstick cooking spray.

2. Combine flour, pecans, oats, raisins, brown sugar, baking powder, cinnamon, baking soda, ginger and salt in large bowl; mix well. Cut in butter with pastry blender or two knives until mixture is crumbly.

3. Add half-and-half by ¼ cupfuls; stir gently until dough comes together. Drop dough by ¼ cupfuls 1 inch apart onto prepared baking sheet. Sprinkle with granulated sugar.

4. Bake 15 to 17 minutes or until golden brown. Cool on baking sheet 5 minutes; remove to wire rack. Serve warm or at room temperature.

Essential Yeast Bread

Sandwich Bread

Makes 2 loaves

½ cup milk

3 tablespoons sugar

2 teaspoons salt

3 tablespoons butter

2 packages (¼ ounce each) active dry yeast

1½ cups warm water (105° to 115°F)

5 to 6 cups all-purpose flour, divided

1. Combine milk, sugar, salt and butter in small saucepan; heat over low heat until butter melts and sugar dissolves. Cool to lukewarm (about 105°F).

2. Dissolve yeast in warm water in large bowl of stand mixer. Add lukewarm milk mixture and 3 cups flour; mix with dough hook at low speed 2 minutes. Add remaining flour, ½ cup at a time; mix until soft dough forms. Mix about 5 minutes or until dough is slightly sticky and elastic.

3. Shape dough into a ball. Place dough in greased bowl; turn to grease top. Cover and let rise in warm place about 1 hour or until doubled in size.

4. Spray two 8×4-inch loaf pans with nonstick cooking spray. Punch down dough. Divide dough in half; shape each half into a loaf. Place in prepared pans; cover and let rise in warm place about 1 hour or until doubled in size. Preheat oven to 400°F.

5. Bake 30 minutes or until golden brown. Remove to wire racks to cool completely.

Whole Wheat Herb Bread

Makes 4 small loaves

⅔ cup water

⅔ cup milk

2 teaspoons sugar

2 packages (¼ ounce each) active dry yeast

3 egg whites, lightly beaten

3 tablespoons olive oil

1 teaspoon salt

½ teaspoon dried basil

½ teaspoon dried oregano

4 to 4½ cups whole wheat flour, divided

1. Bring water to a boil in small saucepan. Remove from heat; stir in milk and sugar. When mixture cools to 110° to 115°F, stir in yeast; let stand 10 minutes or until bubbly.

2. Combine egg whites, oil, salt, basil and oregano in large bowl of stand mixer; beat at medium speed with paddle attachment until blended. Add yeast mixture; mix well. Add 1½ cups flour; beat 2 minutes.

3. Replace paddle attachment with dough hook. Add 2½ cups flour, ½ cup at a time; mix at low speed until dough forms a rough ball. Add enough remaining flour, 1 tablespoon at a time, if necessary to clean side of bowl. Mix at low speed 5 to 7 minutes or until dough is smooth and elastic.

4. Shape dough into a ball. Place dough in greased bowl; turn to grease top. Cover and let rise in warm place about 1 hour or until doubled in size.

5. Preheat oven to 350°F. Line baking sheet with parchment paper. Punch down dough; turn out onto lightly floured surface. Divide dough into four pieces; roll each piece into a ball. Place on prepared baking sheet.

6. Bake 30 to 35 minutes or until golden brown and breads sound hollow when tapped. Remove to wire racks to cool completely.

New York Rye Bread

Makes 2 loaves

2 cups warm water
(105° to 115°F)

⅓ cup packed brown sugar

2 tablespoons vegetable oil

1 tablespoon salt

1 package (¼ ounce)
active dry yeast

2 to 2½ cups bread flour,
divided

1 tablespoon caraway seeds

2 cups rye flour

1 cup whole wheat flour

Cornmeal

1. Combine warm water, brown sugar, oil, salt and yeast in large bowl of stand mixer; stir until yeast is dissolved.

2. Add 2 cups bread flour and caraway seeds; mix with dough hook at low speed 2 minutes. Add rye flour and whole wheat flour, ½ cup at a time; mix until dough begins to form a ball. Add enough remaining bread flour, 1 tablespoon at a time, if necessary to prevent sticking. Mix at low speed 5 to 7 minutes or until dough is smooth and elastic.

3. Shape dough into a ball. Place dough in greased bowl; turn to grease top. Cover and let rise in warm place 1½ to 2 hours or until doubled in size.

4. Line large baking sheet with parchment paper; sprinkle with cornmeal. Punch down dough. Divide dough in half; shape each half into 10-inch oblong-shaped loaf. Place on prepared baking sheet. Cover and let rise in warm place 45 to 60 minutes or until almost doubled in size. Preheat oven to 375°F.

5. Spray or brush loaf with cool water. Cut four ¼-inch-deep slashes in top of each loaf with serrated knife.

6. Bake 25 to 30 minutes or until breads sound hollow when tapped. Remove to wire racks to cool completely.

Crunchy Whole Grain Bread

Makes 2 loaves

2 cups warm water (105° to 115°F), divided

⅓ cup honey

2 tablespoons vegetable oil

1 tablespoon salt

2 packages (¼ ounce each) active dry yeast

2 to 2½ cups whole wheat flour, divided

1 cup bread flour

1¼ cups quick oats, divided

½ cup hulled pumpkin seeds or sunflower kernels

½ cup assorted grains and seeds

1 egg white

1 tablespoon water

1. Combine 1½ cups warm water, honey, oil and salt in small saucepan; heat over low heat until warm (115° to 120°F), stirring occasionally.

2. Dissolve yeast in remaining ½ cup warm water in large bowl of stand mixer; let stand 5 minutes. Stir in honey mixture. Add 1 cup whole wheat flour and bread flour; mix with dough hook at low speed 2 minutes. Slowly add 1 cup oats, pumpkin seeds and assorted grains; mix until incorporated. Add remaining whole wheat flour, ½ cup at a time; mix until dough begins to form a ball. Mix 6 to 8 minutes or until dough is smooth and elastic.

3. Place dough in greased bowl; turn to grease top. Cover and let rise in warm place 1½ to 2 hours or until doubled in size.

4. Spray two 9×5-inch loaf pans with nonstick cooking spray. Punch down dough. Divide dough in half; shape each half into a loaf. Place in prepared pans. Cover and let rise in warm place 1 hour or until almost doubled in size.

5. Preheat oven to 375°F. Beat egg white and 1 tablespoon water in small bowl. Brush over tops of loaves; sprinkle with remaining ¼ cup oats.

6. Bake 35 to 45 minutes or until breads sound hollow when tapped. Cool in pans 10 minutes; remove to wire racks to cool completely.

Rustic White Bread

Makes 1 loaf

5 cups all-purpose flour

2 cups warm water
(105° to 115°F)

1 tablespoon salt

1 package (¼ ounce) instant
or active dry yeast

1. Combine flour and warm water in large bowl; stir to form shaggy dough. Cover with clean kitchen towel; let stand 30 minutes to hydrate flour.

2. Sprinkle salt and yeast over dough; squeeze and fold with hands to incorporate. Turn out dough onto lightly floured surface; knead 2 minutes, adding additional flour by teaspoonfuls if needed (dough will be sticky). Shape dough into a ball; return to bowl. Cover and let rise 2 hours.

3. Gently fold edges of dough to center, pressing down lightly to form a ball. Turn dough over; cover and let rise 3 to 4 hours or until dough has large air bubbles.

4. Turn oven to 450°F; place 5- to 6-quart Dutch oven with lid in oven. Preheat oven and pot 30 minutes. Meanwhile, gently ease dough from bowl onto work surface with lightly floured hands, trying not to tear as much as possible (do not punch down dough). Wrap your hands around sides of dough and gently pull it across work surface to form a ball. Repeat until dough is a smooth ball. Lightly dust medium bowl with flour; place dough in bowl. Cover and let rise while oven is preheating.

5. Use oven mitts to carefully remove Dutch oven from oven and remove lid (pot and lid will be very hot). Gently turn out dough onto work surface; place in Dutch oven, bottom side up. Replace lid using oven mitts; return Dutch oven to oven.

6. Bake bread, covered, 30 minutes. Carefully remove lid; bake 10 to 12 minutes or until top is deep golden brown. Remove to wire rack to cool completely.

Savory Vegetable Oat Bread

Makes 2 loaves

1 tablespoon olive oil

½ cup finely chopped onion

2 cups whole wheat flour

4¼ to 4½ cups all-purpose flour, divided

2 cups old-fashioned oats

¼ cup sugar

2 packages (¼ ounce each) instant yeast

1½ teaspoons salt

1½ cups water

1¼ cups milk

¼ cup (½ stick) butter

1 cup finely shredded carrots

3 tablespoons dried parsley flakes

1 tablespoon butter, melted

1. Heat oil in small skillet over medium heat. Add onion; cook and stir 3 minutes or until softened.

2. Combine whole wheat flour, 1 cup all-purpose flour, oats, sugar, yeast and salt in large bowl of stand mixer; mix well. Combine water, milk and ¼ cup butter in medium saucepan; heat over low heat to 120° to 130°F. Add to flour mixture; beat with paddle attachment at low speed until blended. Beat at medium speed 3 minutes.

3. Replace paddle attachment with dough hook. Add carrots, onion, parsley flakes and 3¼ cups all-purpose flour; mix 5 minutes or until dough is no longer sticky, adding remaining all-purpose flour by tablespoonful, if necessary.

4. Place dough in large greased bowl; turn to grease top. Cover and let rise in warm place about 30 minutes or until doubled in size. Punch down dough; cover and let rest 10 minutes.

5. Spray two 8×4-inch loaf pans with nonstick cooking spray. Shape dough into two loaves; place in prepared pans. Brush with melted butter. Cover and let rise in warm place 30 minutes or until doubled in size. Preheat oven to 350°F.

6. Bake 40 to 45 minutes or until breads sound hollow when tapped. Remove to wire racks to cool completely.

Farmer-Style Sour Cream Bread

Makes 1 loaf

1 cup sour cream

3 tablespoons water

2½ to 3 cups all-purpose flour, divided

1 package (¼ ounce) active dry yeast

2 tablespoons sugar

1½ teaspoons salt

¼ teaspoon baking soda

1 teaspoon vegetable oil

1 tablespoon sesame or poppy seeds

1. Combine sour cream and water in small saucepan; heat over low heat to 110° to 120°F.

2. Combine 2 cups flour, yeast, sugar, salt and baking soda in large bowl of stand mixer. Add sour cream mixture; mix with dough hook at low speed 3 minutes. Add remaining flour, ¼ cup at a time; mix 5 minutes or until dough is smooth and elastic.

3. Line baking sheet with parchment paper. Shape dough into a ball; place on prepared baking sheet. Flatten into 8-inch circle. Brush top with oil; sprinkle with sesame seeds. Cover and let rise in warm place 1 hour or until doubled in size. Preheat oven to 350°F.

4. Bake 22 to 27 minutes or until golden brown. Remove to wire rack to cool completely.

Three-Grain Bread

Makes 1 loaf

1 cup whole wheat flour

¾ cup all-purpose flour

1 package (¼ ounce) instant yeast

1 cup milk

2 tablespoons honey

1 tablespoon olive oil

1 teaspoon salt

½ cup plus 1 tablespoon old-fashioned oats, divided

¼ cup whole grain cornmeal

1 egg beaten with 1 tablespoon water

1. Combine whole wheat flour, all-purpose flour and yeast in large bowl of stand mixer. Combine milk, honey, oil and salt in small saucepan; heat over low heat until warm (110° to 120°F). Add to flour mixture; beat with paddle attachment at medium-high speed 3 minutes. Add ½ cup oats and cornmeal; beat at low speed until blended. If dough is too wet, add additional flour by teaspoonfuls until it begins to come together.

2. Replace paddle attachment with dough hook; mix at low speed 5 minutes or until dough forms a ball. Place dough in large greased bowl; turn to grease top. Cover and let rise in warm place about 1 hour or until dough is puffy and does not spring back when touched.

3. Punch down dough. Shape dough into 8-inch loaf; place on baking sheet lightly sprinkled with cornmeal. Cover and let rise in warm place about 45 minutes or until almost doubled in size. Preheat oven to 375°F.

4. Make shallow slash down center of loaf with sharp knife. Brush lightly with egg mixture; sprinkle with remaining 1 tablespoon oats.

5. Bake 30 minutes or until bread sounds hollow when tapped (internal temperature of 200°F). Remove to wire rack to cool completely.

Oatmeal Honey Bread

Makes 1 loaf

1½ to 2 cups all-purpose flour

1 cup plus 1 tablespoon old-fashioned oats, divided

½ cup whole wheat flour

1 package (¼ ounce) instant yeast

1 teaspoon salt

1⅓ cups plus 1 tablespoon water, divided

¼ cup honey

2 tablespoons butter

1 egg

1. Combine 1½ cups all-purpose flour, 1 cup oats, whole wheat flour, yeast and salt in large bowl of stand mixer.

2. Combine 1⅓ cups water, honey and butter in small saucepan; heat over low heat until honey dissolves and butter melts. Let cool to 130°F (temperature of very hot tap water). Add to flour mixture; beat with paddle attachment at medium speed 2 minutes. Add additional all-purpose flour by tablespoonfuls until dough begins to cling together. Dough should be shaggy and very sticky, not dry. (Dough should not form a ball and/or clean side of bowl.)

3. Replace paddle attachment with dough hook; mix at low speed 4 minutes. Place dough in greased bowl; turn to grease top. Cover and let rise in warm place 45 minutes or until doubled in size.

4. Spray 8×4-inch loaf pan with nonstick cooking spray. Punch down dough; turn out onto floured work surface. Flatten and stretch dough into 8-inch-long oval. Bring long sides together and pinch to seal; fold over short ends and pinch to seal. Place dough seam side down in prepared pan. Cover and let rise in warm place 20 to 30 minutes or until dough reaches top of pan.

5. Preheat oven to 375°F. Beat egg and remaining 1 tablespoon water in small bowl. Brush top of loaf with egg mixture; sprinkle with remaining 1 tablespoon oats.

6. Bake 30 to 35 minutes or until bread sounds hollow when tapped (internal temperature of 190°F). Cool in pan 10 minutes; remove to wire rack to cool completely.

French Cheese Bread

Makes 1 loaf

1 package (¼ ounce)
   active dry yeast

1 teaspoon sugar

4 to 6 tablespoons warm
   water (105° to 115°F)

2½ cups all-purpose flour

¼ cup (½ stick) butter,
   at room temperature

1 teaspoon salt

2 eggs

4 ounces Emmentaler,
   Gruyère or sharp
   Cheddar cheese,
   shredded

1 teaspoon vegetable oil

1. Dissolve yeast and sugar in 4 tablespoons warm water in small bowl; let stand 5 minutes or until bubbly.

2. Combine flour, butter and salt in food processor; process 15 seconds or until blended. Add yeast mixture and eggs; process 15 seconds or just until blended.

3. With motor running, slowly drizzle just enough water through feed tube so dough forms a ball that cleans side of bowl. Process until ball turns around bowl about 25 times. Let dough rest 1 to 2 minutes. With motor running, drizzle in enough remaining water to make dough soft, smooth and satiny. Process until dough turns around bowl about 15 times.

4. Turn out dough onto lightly floured surface; shape into a ball. Place dough in greased bowl; turn to grease top. Cover and let rise in warm place about 1 hour or until doubled in size.

5. Spray 9-inch round cake pan or pie plate with nonstick cooking spray. Punch down dough. Place dough on lightly greased surface; knead cheese into dough. Roll or pat into 8-inch circle; brush with oil. Let rise in warm place about 45 minutes or until doubled in size. Preheat oven to 375°F.

6. Bake 30 to 35 minutes or until browned and bread sounds hollow when tapped. Remove to wire rack to cool completely.

Sweet & Savory Yeast Breads

Oatmeal Raisin Nut Bread

Makes 1 loaf

2 to 2½ cups bread flour, divided

1 cup old-fashioned oats

1 package (¼ ounce) instant yeast

1½ teaspoons salt

1½ teaspoons ground cinnamon

1 cup plus 2 tablespoons warm water (120°F)

¼ cup maple syrup

2 tablespoons vegetable oil

1 cup raisins

¾ cup chopped pecans

1. Combine 1 cup flour, oats, yeast, salt and cinnamon in large bowl of stand mixer. Combine warm water, maple syrup and oil in medium bowl; mix well. Add to flour mixture; beat with paddle attachment at medium speed 3 minutes.

2. Replace paddle attachment with dough hook. Add enough remaining flour, ½ cup at a time, to form soft dough. Mix at low speed 6 minutes or until dough is smooth and elastic. Add raisins and pecans; mix until well incorporated. Shape dough into a ball. Place dough in greased bowl; turn to grease top. Cover and let rise in warm place about 40 minutes or until doubled in size.

3. Spray 9×5-inch loaf pan with nonstick cooking spray. Punch down dough. Roll out dough into 14×8-inch rectangle on lightly floured surface. Starting with short side, tightly roll up dough jelly-roll style; pinch seam to seal. Place seam side down in prepared pan. Cover and let rise about 30 minutes or until doubled in size. Preheat oven to 375°F.

4. Bake 30 to 40 minutes or until top is browned and loaf sounds hollow when tapped (internal temperature of 190°F).

Pecan Sticky Buns

Makes 12 buns

3 to 3½ cups all-purpose flour

⅓ cup nonfat dry milk powder

1 package (¼ ounce) instant yeast

1 teaspoon salt

1 cup water

2 tablespoons honey

1 egg, beaten

½ cup (1 stick) plus 5 tablespoons butter, melted, divided

¾ cup packed brown sugar, divided

3 tablespoons light corn syrup

¾ cup chopped pecans

2 teaspoons ground cinnamon

1. Combine 3 cups flour, milk powder, yeast and salt in large bowl of stand mixer. Combine water and honey in small saucepan; heat over medium heat to 120°F, stirring to dissolve honey. Add to flour mixture; beat with paddle attachment at low speed until blended. Beat in egg and 3 tablespoons melted butter until soft dough forms.

2. Replace paddle attachment with dough hook. Add enough remaining flour, 1 tablespoon at a time, if necessary to prevent sticking. Mix at low speed 5 minutes or until dough is smooth and elastic. Shape dough into a ball. Place dough in large greased bowl; turn to grease top. Cover and let rise in warm place 30 to 40 minutes or until doubled in size.

3. Meanwhile, combine ½ cup butter, ½ cup brown sugar and corn syrup in small saucepan; cook and stir over medium heat until melted and smooth. Pour into bottom of 9-inch round cake pan; sprinkle with pecans. Combine remaining ¼ cup brown sugar and cinnamon in small bowl; mix well.

4. Punch down dough. Roll out dough into 15×9-inch rectangle on floured surface. Brush with remaining 2 tablespoons butter; sprinkle with cinnamon-sugar. Starting with long side, roll up dough jelly-roll style; pinch seam to seal. Cut crosswise into 12 (1¼-inch) slices; arrange slices cut sides up in prepared pan. Cover and let rise in warm place 25 minutes. Preheat oven to 350°F.

5. Bake 30 minutes or until golden brown. Cool in pan 2 minutes; invert onto plate.

Walnut Fig Bread

Makes 1 loaf

1 cup honey beer or water

2 tablespoons butter or olive oil

1 tablespoon honey

2¼ cups all-purpose flour, divided

1 cup whole wheat flour

1 package (¼ ounce) active dry yeast

1 tablespoon fennel seeds

1½ teaspoons salt

1 egg, beaten

1 cup chopped dried figs

½ cup chopped walnuts, toasted

*To toast walnuts, cook in medium skillet over medium heat 2 minutes or until lightly browned, stirring frequently.

1. Combine beer, butter and honey in small saucepan; heat over low heat to 120°F.

2. Combine 1 cup all-purpose flour, whole wheat flour, yeast, fennel seeds and salt in large bowl of stand mixer. Add beer mixture; beat with paddle attachment at medium-low speed 3 minutes. Add egg; beat until blended.

3. Replace paddle attachment with dough hook. Add remaining all-purpose flour, ¼ cup at a time; mix at low speed to form soft dough. Add figs and walnuts; mix about 5 minutes or until dough is smooth and elastic.

4. Shape dough into a ball. Place dough in greased bowl; turn to grease top. Cover and let rise in warm place about 1 hour or until doubled in size.

5. Line baking sheet with parchment paper. Punch down dough. Shape dough into round loaf; place on prepared baking sheet. Cover and let rise in warm place 40 minutes or until doubled in size. Preheat oven to 350°F.

6. Bake 30 to 35 minutes or until golden brown and bread sounds hollow when tapped. Remove to wire rack to cool completely.

Pull-Apart Garlic Cheese Bread

Makes 12 servings

3 cups all-purpose flour

1 package (¼ ounce) instant yeast

1 teaspoon salt

1 cup warm water (120°F)

2 tablespoons olive oil

6 cloves garlic, minced, divided

¼ cup (½ stick) butter

¼ teaspoon paprika

1 cup grated Parmesan cheese

1 cup (4 ounces) shredded mozzarella cheese

½ cup pizza sauce

Chopped fresh parsley (optional)

1. Combine flour, yeast and salt in large bowl of stand mixer. Stir in water and oil with spoon or spatula to form rough dough. Add half of garlic; mix with dough hook at low speed 5 to 7 minutes or until dough is smooth and elastic.

2. Shape dough into a ball. Place in greased bowl; turn to grease top. Cover and let rise in warm place 45 minutes to 1 hour or until doubled in size.

3. Melt butter in small skillet over medium-low heat. Add remaining garlic; cook and stir 1 minute. Stir in paprika; remove from heat. Brush 9-inch springform pan with some of butter mixture. Place 6-ounce ramekin in center of pan. Place Parmesan in shallow bowl.

4. Turn out dough onto lightly floured surface; pat into 9-inch square. Cut into 1-inch squares; roll each square into a ball. Dip half of balls in melted butter mixture; roll in Parmesan to coat. Place around ramekin in prepared pan; sprinkle with ½ cup mozzarella. Repeat with remaining dough, butter mixture, Parmesan and mozzarella. Cover and let rise in warm place 1 hour or until dough has risen to top of pan.

5. Preheat oven to 350°F. Line baking sheet with foil. Pour pizza sauce into ramekin. Place springform pan on prepared baking sheet.

6. Bake 20 to 25 minutes or until bread is firm and golden brown. Loosen edges of bread with knife; carefully remove side of pan. Sprinkle with parsley, if desired. Serve warm.

Cinnamon Raisin Bread

Makes 1 loaf

1 cup milk

3 tablespoons butter

3 to 3½ cups all-purpose
flour, divided

½ cup sugar, divided

1 package (¼ ounce)
instant yeast

1 teaspoon salt

1 whole egg

1 egg, separated

1 teaspoon vanilla

¾ cup raisins

1 tablespoon ground
cinnamon

1 tablespoon butter, melted

1 tablespoon water

1. Combine milk and 3 tablespoons butter in small saucepan; heat over low heat to 115° to 120°F (butter does not need to melt completely).

2. Combine 1½ cups flour, ¼ cup sugar, yeast and salt in large bowl of stand mixer. Slowly add milk mixture; beat with paddle attachment at low speed until blended. Beat at medium speed 2 minutes. Add whole egg, egg yolk and vanilla; beat 2 minutes.

3. Replace paddle attachment with dough hook. Add 1½ cups flour; mix at low speed to form soft dough. Mix 5 minutes or until dough is smooth and elastic, adding enough remaining flour, 1 tablespoon at a time, if necessary to clean side of bowl. Add raisins; mix until incorporated. Shape dough into a ball. Place dough in greased bowl; turn to grease top. Cover and let rise in warm place about 1 hour or until doubled in size.

4. Punch down dough; knead on lightly floured surface 1 minute. Cover and let rest 10 minutes. Spray 9×5-inch loaf pan with nonstick cooking spray. Combine remaining ¼ cup sugar and cinnamon in small bowl; reserve 1 teaspoon mixture for top of loaf, if desired.

5. Roll out dough into 20×9-inch rectangle with lightly floured rolling pin. Brush with 1 tablespoon melted butter; sprinkle with remaining cinnamon-sugar. Starting with short side, roll up dough jelly-roll style; pinch seam and ends to seal. Place loaf, seam side down, in prepared pan; cover and let rise in warm place about 30 minutes or until doubled in size.

6. Preheat oven to 375°F. Beat egg white and water in small bowl until blended. Brush over top of loaf; sprinkle with reserved cinnamon-sugar.

7. Bake 40 to 45 minutes or until bread sounds hollow when tapped (internal temperature of 190°F). Cover loosely with foil halfway through baking time if bread is browning too fast. Remove to wire rack to cool completely.

Irish Speckled Loaf

Makes 2 loaves

¾ cup plus 1 tablespoon water, divided

¾ cup milk

¼ cup (½ stick) butter, softened

4 to 4½ cups all-purpose flour

½ cup plus 1 teaspoon sugar, divided

1 package (¼ ounce) instant yeast

1 teaspoon salt

½ teaspoon ground cinnamon

¼ teaspoon ground nutmeg

1 egg

1 cup golden raisins (optional)

½ cup chopped dried or candied fruit (apricots, cherries, prunes, etc.)

1. Combine ¾ cup water, milk and butter in small saucepan; heat over low heat until butter melts and temperature reaches 120° to 130°F.

2. Combine 4 cups flour, ½ cup sugar, yeast, salt, cinnamon and nutmeg in large bowl of stand mixer. Add milk mixture; beat with paddle attachment at medium speed 2 minutes or until well blended. Beat in egg.

3. Replace paddle attachment with dough hook. Add enough remaining flour, 1 tablespoon at a time, mixing at low speed to form slightly sticky dough. Mix 4 minutes or until dough is smooth and elastic. Shape dough into a ball. Place dough in greased bowl; turn to grease top. Cover and let rise in warm place 45 minutes to 1 hour or until doubled in size.

4. Spray two 8×4-inch loaf pans with nonstick cooking spray. Punch down dough; turn out onto floured surface. Knead in raisins, if desired, and dried fruit. Divide dough in half; shape each half into a ball. Cover and let rest 5 minutes. To shape loaves, flatten and stretch each ball of dough into oval shape. Bring long sides together and pinch to seal; fold over short ends and pinch to seal. Place seam side down in prepared pans. Cover and let rise 45 minutes or until dough almost reaches tops of pans. Preheat oven to 375°F.

5. Bake 35 to 40 minutes or until browned. (Cover loosely with foil if breads are browning too fast.) Dissolve remaining 1 teaspoon sugar in 1 tablespoon water in small bowl. Brush over loaves; bake 2 minutes. Cool in pans 2 minutes; remove to wire racks to cool 30 minutes. Serve warm.

Asiago-Pepper Bread
Makes 1 loaf

2½ to 3 cups bread flour or
　　all-purpose flour, divided

¼ cup yellow cornmeal

1 package (¼ ounce)
　　active dry yeast

2 teaspoons coarsely
　　ground black pepper

1 teaspoon salt

1 cup warm water
　　(105° to 115°F)

1 tablespoon vegetable oil

1 cup (4 ounces) shredded
　　Asiago cheese

1 egg white

1 tablespoon water

1. Combine 1 cup flour, cornmeal, yeast, pepper and salt in large bowl of stand mixer. Add warm water and oil; beat with paddle attachment at low speed 30 seconds. Beat at medium speed 5 minutes. Add cheese and ½ cup flour; beat until blended.

2. Replace paddle attachment with dough hook. Add remaining flour, ¼ cup at a time, to form soft dough. Mix at low speed about 5 minutes or until dough is smooth and elastic. Shape dough into a ball. Place dough in greased bowl; turn to grease top. Cover and let rise in warm place about 1 hour 15 minutes or until doubled in size.

3. Punch down dough; turn out onto lightly floured surface. Cover and let rest 10 minutes. Line baking sheet with parchment paper.

4. Roll out dough into 15×7-inch rectangle. Starting with long side, roll up jelly-roll style. Pinch seam to seal; slightly stretch ends to taper. Place loaf on prepared baking sheet.

5. Beat egg white and 1 tablespoon water in small bowl until blended; brush over top of loaf. Cover loosely and let rise in warm place about 45 minutes or until almost doubled in size. Preheat oven to 350°F.

6. Use sharp knife to make six to eight shallow diagonal cuts in top of loaf. Bake 20 minutes. Brush top of loaf with some of remaining egg white mixture. Bake 15 to 20 minutes or until bread sounds hollow when tapped. Remove to wire rack to cool completely.

Apricot Cranberry Bread

Makes 1 loaf

- ½ cup dried apricots, chopped
- ½ cup dried cranberries, chopped
- 3 tablespoons orange juice
- ⅔ cup milk
- 6 tablespoons (¾ stick) butter, softened
- 2½ to 3 cups all-purpose flour, divided

- ¼ cup sugar
- 1 package (¼ ounce) active dry yeast
- ¾ teaspoon salt
- ½ teaspoon ground ginger
- ½ teaspoon ground nutmeg
- 2 eggs, divided
- ½ cup pecans, toasted and coarsely chopped
- 1 teaspoon water

1. Combine apricots, cranberries and orange juice in medium microwavable bowl; cover and microwave on HIGH 25 to 35 seconds to soften. Set aside to cool.

2. Combine milk and butter in small saucepan; heat over low heat to 120°F. Combine 1½ cups flour, sugar, yeast, salt, ginger and nutmeg in large bowl of stand mixer. Slowly add milk mixture; beat with paddle attachment at low speed until blended. Add 1 egg; beat 2 minutes or until blended. Replace paddle attachment with dough hook. Add 1 cup flour, ¼ cup at a time; mix at low speed 2 minutes or until dough is no longer sticky. Add remaining flour, 1 tablespoon at a time, to prevent sticking, if necessary. Mix 5 minutes or until dough is smooth and elastic.

3. Turn out dough onto floured surface. Drain or blot apricot mixture; stir in pecans. Flatten dough into ¾-inch-thick rectangle; sprinkle with one third of fruit mixture. Starting from short side, roll up dough jelly-roll style. Repeat flattening, sprinkling and rolling process twice using remaining fruit mixture. Knead until blended. Shape dough into a ball. Place dough in greased bowl; turn to grease top. Cover and let rise 1 hour or until doubled in size.

4. Spray 9-inch round cake pan or pie plate with nonstick cooking spray. Punch down dough. Pat dough into 8-inch circle; place in prepared pan. Cover loosely and let rise 1 hour or until doubled in size.

5. Preheat oven to 375°F. Beat remaining egg and 1 teaspoon water in small bowl until blended; brush over top of loaf.

6. Bake 30 to 35 minutes or until bread sounds hollow when tapped. Remove to wire rack to cool completely.

Bacon Cheddar Monkey Bread

Makes 12 servings

1¾ cups (7 ounces) shredded sharp Cheddar cheese

12 ounces bacon, crisp-cooked and chopped (about 1 cup)

¼ cup finely chopped green onions

2¾ to 3 cups all-purpose flour, divided

1 package (¼ ounce) instant yeast

1 teaspoon salt

1 cup warm water (120°F)

2 tablespoons olive oil

⅓ cup butter, melted

1 egg

1. Combine cheese, bacon and green onions in medium bowl; mix well.

2. Combine 1½ cups flour, yeast and salt in large bowl of stand mixer. Add warm water and oil; beat with paddle attachment at medium speed 3 minutes.

3. Replace paddle attachment with dough hook. Add 1¼ cups flour; mix at low speed until dough comes together. Add 1 cup cheese mixture; mix 6 to 8 minutes or until dough is smooth and elastic, adding remaining ¼ cup flour if necessary to clean side of bowl. Shape dough into a ball. Place dough in greased bowl; turn to grease top. Cover and let rise in warm place 30 minutes or until doubled in size.

4. Generously spray 12-cup (10-inch) bundt pan with nonstick cooking spray. Whisk butter and egg in shallow bowl until blended.

5. Punch down dough. Roll 1-inch pieces of dough into balls. Dip balls in butter mixture; roll in remaining cheese mixture to coat. Layer balls in prepared pan. Cover and let rise in warm place about 40 minutes or until almost doubled in size. Preheat oven to 375°F.

6. Bake 35 minutes or until golden brown. Loosen edges of bread with knife; invert onto wire rack. Cool 5 minutes; serve warm.

Cinnamon Rolls

Makes 18 rolls

1 package (¼ ounce)
   active dry yeast
1 cup warm water
   (105° to 115°F)
½ cup plus 2 tablespoons
   milk, divided
¼ cup granulated sugar
5 tablespoons butter,
   melted, divided
1 egg
1 teaspoon vanilla

½ teaspoon salt
2½ to 2¾ cups all-purpose
   flour, divided
½ cup packed brown sugar
1 tablespoon ground
   cinnamon
1 teaspoon grated
   orange peel
⅓ cup raisins (optional)
½ cup powdered sugar,
   sifted

1. Dissolve yeast in warm water in large bowl of stand mixer; let stand 5 minutes or until bubbly.

2. Add ½ cup milk, granulated sugar, 2 tablespoons butter, egg, vanilla and salt; beat with paddle attachment at medium speed until blended. Replace paddle attachment with dough hook. Add 2½ cups flour; mix at low speed to form soft dough. Add enough remaining flour, 1 tablespoon at a time, if necessary to prevent sticking. Mix 5 minutes or until dough is smooth and elastic.

3. Shape dough into a ball. Place dough in greased bowl; turn to grease top. Cover and let rise in warm place about 1 hour or until doubled in size.

4. Spray two 8-inch round cake pans with nonstick cooking spray. Combine brown sugar, 1 tablespoon butter, cinnamon and orange peel in small bowl; mix well.

5. Punch down dough. Roll out dough into 18×8-inch rectangle on lightly floured surface. Brush with remaining 2 tablespoons butter; spread with brown sugar mixture. Sprinkle with raisins, if desired. Starting with long side, roll up dough jelly-roll style; pinch seam to seal. Cut crosswise into 1-inch slices; arrange slices cut sides up in prepared pans. Cover loosely and let rise in warm place 30 to 40 minutes or until almost doubled in size. Preheat oven to 350°F.

6. Bake 18 minutes or until golden brown. Remove to wire racks to cool slightly. Meanwhile, whisk powdered sugar and 1 tablespoon milk in small bowl until smooth. Add additional milk, if necessary, to reach desired consistency. Drizzle glaze over warm rolls.

Chili Cheese Bread

Makes 1 loaf

2 tablespoons butter

½ cup finely chopped onion

1 clove garlic, minced

¾ cup milk

2¾ cups bread flour, divided

1 tablespoon sugar

1 package (¼ ounce) instant yeast

2 to 3 teaspoons chili powder

1 teaspoon salt

1 teaspoon dried basil

1 egg

1¼ cups (5 ounces) shredded sharp Cheddar cheese

1. Melt butter in medium saucepan over medium heat. Add onion and garlic; cook and stir 5 minutes or until onion is tender. Add milk; heat to 120°F.

2. Combine 1 cup flour, sugar, yeast, chili powder, salt and basil in large bowl of stand mixer. Add milk mixture; beat with paddle attachment at medium speed 2 minutes. Add egg; beat 1 minute.

3. Replace paddle attachment with dough hook. Add 1 cup flour and cheese; mix at low speed 2 minutes. Add enough remaining flour, ¼ cup at a time, to form firm dough. Mix 5 minutes or until dough is smooth and elastic.

4. Shape dough into a ball. Place dough in greased bowl; turn to grease top. Cover and let rise in warm place about 30 minutes or until doubled in size.

5. Spray 9×5-inch loaf pan with nonstick cooking spray. Punch down dough. Shape dough into a loaf; place in prepared pan. Cover and let rise in warm place about 20 minutes or until doubled in size. Preheat oven to 375°F.

6. Bake 30 to 35 minutes or until browned and bread sounds hollow when tapped.

Honey Butter Pull-Apart Bread

Makes 1 loaf

3 **cups all-purpose flour**

1 **package (¼ ounce) instant yeast**

1 **teaspoon salt**

1 **cup warm water (120°F)**

2 **tablespoons butter, melted**

¼ **cup (½ stick) butter, softened**

¼ **cup honey**

1. Combine flour, yeast and salt in large bowl of stand mixer. Stir in warm water and melted butter with spoon or spatula to form rough dough. Mix with dough hook at low speed 5 to 7 minutes or until dough is smooth and elastic.

2. Shape dough into a ball. Place in greased bowl; turn to grease top. Cover and let rise in warm place 45 minutes to 1 hour or until doubled in size.

3. Spray 8×4-inch loaf pan with nonstick cooking spray. Combine softened butter and honey in small bowl; mix well.

4. Turn out dough onto lightly floured surface. Roll out dough into 18×10-inch rectangle; cut in half crosswise to make two 9×10-inch rectangles. Spread some of honey butter over one half of dough; top with remaining half. Cut dough in half crosswise to make two 9×5-inch rectangles. Spread some of honey butter over one half; top with remaining half. Cut dough in half lengthwise, then cut crosswise into 1-inch strips. Place rows of strips vertically in prepared pan. Cover and let rise in warm place 1 hour or until dough is puffy. Preheat oven to 350°F. Brush or dollop remaining honey butter over dough strips.

5. Bake 30 minutes or until bread is firm and golden brown. Remove to wire rack to cool slightly. Serve warm.

Pizza & Flatbreads

Quattro Formaggio Focaccia

Makes 1 focaccia

1 tablespoon sugar

1 package (¼ ounce) instant yeast

1¼ cups warm water (105° to 115°F)

3 to 3¼ cups all-purpose flour

¼ cup plus 2 tablespoons olive oil, divided

1 teaspoon salt

¼ cup marinara sauce with basil

1 cup (4 ounces) shredded Italian cheese blend

1. Dissolve sugar and yeast in warm water in large bowl of stand mixer; let stand 5 minutes or until bubbly. Stir in 3 cups flour, ¼ cup oil and salt with spoon or spatula to form rough dough. Mix with dough hook at low speed 5 minutes, adding additional flour, 1 tablespoon at a time, if necessary for dough to come together. (Dough will be sticky and will not clean side of bowl.)

2. Shape dough into a ball. Place dough in large greased bowl; turn to grease top. Cover and let rise 1 to 1½ hours or until doubled in size.

3. Punch down dough. Pour remaining 2 tablespoons oil into 13×9-inch baking pan; pat and stretch dough to fill pan. Make indentations in top of dough with fingertips.

4. Spread marinara sauce evenly over dough; sprinkle with cheese. Cover and let rise 30 minutes or until puffy. Preheat oven to 425°F.

5. Bake 17 to 20 minutes or until golden brown. Cut into squares or strips.

Easy Mushroom Pizza

Makes 2 pizzas (8 servings)

3 to 3½ cups all-purpose flour

1¼ cups warm water (120°F)

3 tablespoons olive oil, divided

1 package (¼ ounce) instant yeast

1¼ teaspoons salt, divided

8 to 10 medium mushrooms, cut into ⅛-inch-thick slices

⅛ teaspoon black pepper

1 cup pizza sauce, divided

3 cups (12 ounces) shredded mozzarella cheese, divided

Pinch dried oregano and red pepper flakes

Fresh thyme and/or chopped fresh basil (optional)

1. Combine 3 cups flour, water, 2 tablespoons oil, yeast and 1 teaspoon salt in large bowl of stand mixer. Mix with dough hook at low speed about 2 minutes or until soft dough forms, adding additional flour, 1 tablespoon at a time, if necessary to clean side of bowl. Mix at medium-low speed 5 minutes.

2. Shape dough into a ball. Place dough in greased bowl; turn to grease top. Cover and let rise in warm place about 1 hour or until doubled in size.

3. Preheat oven to 500°F. Combine mushrooms, 1 teaspoon oil, remaining ¼ teaspoon salt and pepper in small bowl; toss to coat.

4. Gently punch down dough; turn out onto lightly floured surface. Divide dough in half; keep one half covered to prevent drying out. Roll out remaining half of dough into 12-inch circle; transfer to pizza pan or baking sheet.

5. Brush edge of dough with 1 teaspoon oil. Spread ½ cup sauce over dough, leaving ¼-inch border. Sprinkle with 1½ cups cheese; top with half of mushrooms. Sprinkle with oregano and red pepper flakes.

6. Bake about 10 minutes or until crust is golden brown and cheese is melted. Sprinkle with fresh herbs, if desired; remove to wire rack to cool 5 minutes. While pizza is baking, roll out and top remaining half of dough with remaining oil, sauce, cheese and mushrooms.

Olive and Herb Focaccia

Makes 2 focaccia

3½ to 3¾ cups bread flour

1¼ cups warm water (120°F)

½ cup extra virgin olive oil, divided

1 package (¼ ounce) instant yeast

2 teaspoons honey

1 teaspoon salt

1 cup chopped pitted kalamata olives

3 tablespoons chopped fresh rosemary

2 tablespoons chopped fresh thyme

3 cloves garlic, minced

Black pepper

¼ cup grated Romano cheese

1. Combine 3½ cups flour, water, 3 tablespoons oil, yeast, honey and 1 teaspoon salt in large bowl of stand mixer. Mix with dough hook at low speed 2 minutes or until soft dough forms, adding additional flour, 1 tablespoon at a time, if necessary to clean side of bowl. Mix 5 minutes or until dough is smooth and elastic.

2. Shape dough into a ball. Place dough in greased bowl; turn to grease top. Cover and let rise in warm place about 1 hour or until doubled in size.

3. Preheat oven to 450°F. Brush each of two 9-inch cake pans or deep-dish pizza pans with 1 tablespoon oil. Divide dough in half. Roll out each half into 9-inch circle on lightly floured surface. Place dough in prepared pans; cover and let rest 10 minutes.

4. Make indentations in top of dough with fingertips or handle of wooden spoon. Sprinkle evenly with olives, rosemary, thyme and garlic; drizzle with remaining 3 tablespoons oil. Sprinkle with additional salt and pepper.

5. Bake about 15 minutes or until lightly browned. Immediately sprinkle with cheese. Remove to wire racks to cool slightly. Serve warm.

Pizza Margherita

Makes 2 pizzas (8 servings)

Dough

- 2 **cups all-purpose flour**
- 1 **cup whole wheat flour**
- 2 **teaspoons salt**
- 1 **package (¼ ounce) instant yeast**
- 1 **cup warm water (120°F)**
- 2 **tablespoons extra virgin olive oil**
- 2 **teaspoons cornmeal**

Sauce*

- 1 **tablespoon olive oil**
- 1 **onion, chopped**
- 2 **cloves garlic, minced**
- 1 **can (about 14 ounces) fire-roasted diced tomatoes**
- ½ **teaspoon Italian seasoning**

Toppings

- 3 to 4 **plum tomatoes, cut into ¼-inch slices**
- 16 **ounces fresh mozzarella cheese, thinly sliced**
- 4 to 6 **leaves fresh basil, torn into pieces**

Or substitute prepared pizza sauce, if desired.

1. For dough, combine all-purpose flour, whole wheat flour, salt and yeast in food processor; pulse just until combined. With motor running, add warm water and 2 tablespoons extra virgin olive oil through feed tube; process 30 seconds or until dough forms a ball. Dough should be slightly sticky. If ball does not form and dough seems too wet, add additional all-purpose flour, 1 tablespoon at a time. If too dry, add additional water, 1 tablespoon at a time.

2. Turn out dough onto floured surface; knead 1 minute. Place dough in greased bowl; turn to grease top. Cover and let rise in warm place 45 minutes or until almost doubled in size.**

3. For sauce, heat 1 tablespoon olive oil in medium saucepan over medium heat. Add onion and garlic; cook and stir 2 minutes or until softened. Add diced tomatoes and Italian seasoning; cook over medium-high heat 5 to 10 minutes or until slightly reduced, stirring occasionally. Remove from heat; let cool. Transfer to food processor; pulse until almost smooth. Refrigerate until ready to use.

4. Preheat oven to 450°F. Sprinkle two baking sheets or pizza pans with cornmeal. Punch down dough. Divide dough in half; roll out each half into 12-inch circle on floured surface with floured rolling pin. Transfer dough to prepared baking sheets.

5. Spread thin layer of sauce over dough, leaving ½-inch border. (Freeze leftover sauce for later use.) Top with plum tomatoes and cheese.

6. Bake 8 to 10 minutes or until crust begins to brown around edges and cheese is bubbly and browned in spots. Remove to cutting board; sprinkle with basil.

**Dough may also be refrigerated for up to 24 hours for a slower rise. Bring dough to room temperature and proceed with recipe. Or wrap and freeze up to 3 months.

Tomato and Cheese Focaccia

Makes 1 focaccia

1 package (¼ ounce)
   active dry yeast

¾ cup warm water
   (105° to 115°F)

2 cups all-purpose flour

½ teaspoon salt

4½ tablespoons olive oil,
   divided

1 teaspoon Italian seasoning

8 oil-packed sun-dried
   tomatoes, well drained

½ cup (2 ounces) shredded
   provolone cheese

¼ cup grated Parmesan
   cheese

1. Dissolve yeast in warm water in small bowl; let stand 5 minutes or until bubbly. Combine flour and salt in food processor. Add yeast mixture and 3 tablespoons oil; process until dough forms a ball. Process 1 minute.

2. Turn dough out onto lightly floured surface. Knead about 2 minutes or until dough is smooth and elastic. Shape dough into a ball. Place dough in greased bowl; turn to grease top. Cover and let rise in warm place about 30 minutes or until doubled in size.

3. Brush 10-inch round cake pan, deep-dish pizza pan or springform pan with ½ tablespoon oil. Punch down dough; let rest 5 minutes.

4. Press dough into prepared pan. Brush with remaining 1 tablespoon oil; sprinkle with Italian seasoning. Press sun-dried tomatoes into top of dough; sprinkle with provolone and Parmesan. Cover and let rise in warm place 15 minutes. Preheat oven to 425°F.

5. Bake 20 to 25 minutes or until golden brown. Cut into wedges.

Serving Suggestion: Serve with rosemary-infused olive oil for dipping.

Naan (Indian Flatbread)

Makes 6 naan

1 package (¼ ounce)
  active dry yeast

1 teaspoon sugar

¼ cup plus 2 tablespoons
  warm water (105° to
  115°F), divided

3 cups all-purpose flour

1 teaspoon salt

1 teaspoon kalonji* seeds or
  poppy seeds (optional)

½ cup plain whole milk
  Greek yogurt

¼ cup (½ stick) melted
  butter, plus additional
  butter for brushing
  on naan

*Kalonji seed is often called onion seed or black cumin seed; it is available in Indian markets and is traditional in some varieties of naan.

1. Dissolve yeast and sugar in 2 tablespoons warm water in small bowl; let stand 5 minutes or until bubbly. Combine flour, salt and kalonji, if desired, in large bowl of stand mixer.

2. Add yeast mixture, yogurt and ¼ cup butter; mix with dough hook at low speed until blended. Add remaining ¼ cup water, 1 tablespoon at a time, until dough comes together and cleans side of bowl. (You may not need all the water.) Mix at low speed 5 to 7 minutes or until dough is smooth and elastic.

3. Shape dough into a ball. Place dough in greased bowl; turn to grease top. Cover and let rise in warm place 1½ to 2 hours or until doubled in size.

4. Punch down dough. Divide dough into six pieces; roll each piece into a ball. Place on plate sprayed with nonstick cooking spray; cover and let rest 10 to 15 minutes.

5. Meanwhile, prepare grill for direct cooking or preheat oven to 500°F with baking stone on rack in lower third of oven. (Remove other racks.)

6. Place each ball of dough on lightly floured surface; roll and stretch into ⅛-inch-thick oval. Place on grill or baking stone two or three at a time. Grill, covered, or bake 2 minutes until puffed. Turn, brush tops with butter and grill or bake 1 to 2 minutes or until browned in patches on both sides. Brush bottoms with butter; serve warm.

Focaccia with Roasted Peppers

Makes 1 focaccia

1 package (¼ ounce) active dry yeast

1 teaspoon sugar

1½ cups warm water (105° to 115°F)

4 cups all-purpose flour, divided

7 tablespoons olive oil, divided

1 teaspoon salt

¼ cup bottled roasted red peppers, drained and cut into strips

¼ cup pitted black olives

1. Dissolve yeast and sugar in warm water in large bowl of stand mixer; let stand 5 minutes or until bubbly. Add 3½ cups flour, 3 tablespoons oil and salt; mix with dough hook at low speed until soft dough forms. Add remaining flour, 1 tablespoon at a time, if necessary to prevent sticking. Mix 5 minutes or until dough is smooth and elastic.

2. Shape dough into a ball. Place dough in greased bowl; turn to grease top. Cover and let rise in warm place 1 hour or until doubled in size.

3. Brush 15×10-inch jelly-roll pan with 1 tablespoon oil. Punch down dough; turn out onto lightly floured surface. Flatten dough into rectangle; roll out almost to size of pan. Place dough in pan; gently press dough to edges.

4. Make indentations in top of dough every 1 or 2 inches with fingertips or handle of wooden spoon. Brush with remaining 3 tablespoons oil. Gently press roasted peppers and olives into dough. Cover and let rise in warm place 30 minutes or until doubled in size. Preheat oven to 450°F.

5. Bake 12 to 18 minutes or until golden brown. Cut into squares or rectangles. Serve warm.

Pita Bread

Makes 8 pita breads

3½ **cups all-purpose flour**

1 **tablespoon salt**

1 **tablespoon sugar**

1 **package (¼ ounce) instant yeast**

1½ **cups warm water (120°F)**

2 **tablespoons olive oil**

1. Combine flour, salt, sugar and yeast in large bowl of stand mixer. Add 1½ cups water and oil; stir with spoon or spatula until rough dough forms. If dough appears too dry, add additional 1 to 2 tablespoons water. Mix with dough hook at low speed 5 minutes.

2. Shape dough into a ball. Place dough in greased bowl; turn to grease top. Cover and let rise in warm place 1 hour or until doubled in size.

3. Preheat oven to 500°F. Turn out dough onto lightly floured surface; press into circle. Cut dough into eight wedges. Roll each wedge into a smooth ball; flatten slightly. Let rest 10 minutes.

4. Roll each ball into a circle about ¼ inch thick. Place on two ungreased baking sheets.

5. Bake one baking sheet at a time 5 minutes or until pitas are puffed and set. Remove to wire rack to cool slightly.

Pepperoni Pizza

Makes 1 pizza (4 servings)

1 package (¼ ounce) active dry yeast

½ teaspoon sugar

⅔ cup warm water (105° to 115°F)

2 to 2¼ cups all-purpose flour

2 tablespoons olive oil

½ teaspoon salt

1 teaspoon cornmeal

½ cup pizza sauce

2 cups (8 ounces) shredded mozzarella cheese

18 to 20 slices pepperoni

1. Dissolve yeast and sugar in warm water in large bowl of stand mixer; let stand 5 minutes or until bubbly.

2. Add 2 cups flour, oil and salt; mix with dough hook at low speed 2 minutes or until soft dough forms, adding additional flour, 1 tablespoon at a time, if necessary to clean side of bowl. Mix at low speed 5 minutes.

3. Shape dough into a ball. Place dough in greased bowl; turn to grease top. Cover and let rise in warm place about 1 hour or until doubled in size.

4. Preheat oven to 500°F; place rack in lower third of oven. Sprinkle pizza pan or baking sheet with cornmeal.

5. Gently punch down dough; turn out on lightly floured surface. Roll out dough into 12-inch circle about ¼ inch thick; transfer to prepared pizza pan. Spread sauce over dough, leaving ¼ inch edge uncovered. Top with cheese and pepperoni.

6. Bake about 10 minutes or until crust is golden brown and cheese is melted and beginning to brown in spots. Remove to wire rack to cool 5 minutes.

Tip: For additional flavor, sprinkle dried oregano and black pepper over the pizza before baking.

Flour Tortillas

Makes 12 tortillas

2 **cups all-purpose flour**

¾ **teaspoon salt**

¾ **teaspoon baking powder**

⅔ **cup warm water (105° to 115°F)**

¼ **cup vegetable oil**

1. Combine flour, salt and baking powder in large bowl of stand mixer; mix with dough hook at low speed to combine. With mixer running at medium speed, add water and oil in thin, steady stream. Beat 2 minutes or until dough is well blended and smooth.

2. Turn out dough onto lightly floured surface; divide into 12 pieces. Shape dough into balls. Cover with clean kitchen towel; let rest at least 15 minutes.

3. Heat medium skillet over medium-high heat. Roll each piece of dough into very thin 6-inch circle on lightly floured surface with lightly floured rolling pin. Working with one tortilla at at time, add to hot skillet; cook 1 minute. (Bottom should be golden brown in spots and top should be bubbly.) Turn and cook about 30 seconds or until tortilla is firm and beginning to brown in spots. Stack cooked tortillas; wrap in clean kitchen towel to keep soft and warm.

Note: Tortillas can be stored in a resealable food storage bag or an airtight container at room temperature overnight, or refrigerated up to 1 week.

Smaller Breads

Soft Garlic Breadsticks

Makes about 16 breadsticks

1½ cups water

6 tablespoons (¾ stick) butter, divided

4 cups all-purpose flour

2 tablespoons sugar

1 package (¼ ounce) active dry yeast

1½ teaspoons salt

¾ teaspoon coarse salt

¼ teaspoon garlic powder

1. Heat water and 2 tablespoons butter in small saucepan over medium heat to 110° to 115°F (butter does not need to melt completely).

2. Combine flour, sugar, yeast and 1½ teaspoons salt in large bowl of stand mixer. Add water mixture; mix with dough hook at low speed until dough begins to come together. Mix about 5 minutes or until dough is smooth and elastic. Shape dough into a ball. Place in large greased bowl; turn to grease top. Cover and let rise in warm place about 1 hour or until doubled in size.

3. Line two baking sheets with parchment paper or spray with nonstick cooking spray. Punch down dough. For each breadstick, pull off piece of dough slightly larger than a golf ball (about 2 ounces) and roll between hands or on work surface into 7-inch-long rope. Place on prepared baking sheets; cover loosely and let rise in warm place about 45 minutes or until doubled in size.

4. Preheat oven to 400°F. Melt remaining 4 tablespoons butter in small bowl. Brush breadsticks with 2 tablespoons butter; sprinkle with coarse salt.

5. Bake breadsticks 13 to 15 minutes or until golden brown. Stir garlic powder into remaining 2 tablespoons melted butter; brush over breadsticks immediately after removing from oven. Serve warm.

Pull-Apart Rye Rolls

Makes 24 rolls

¾ cup water

2 tablespoons butter

2 tablespoons molasses

2¼ cups all-purpose flour, divided

½ cup rye flour

⅓ cup nonfat dry milk powder

1 package (¼ ounce) active dry yeast

1½ teaspoons salt

1½ teaspoons caraway seeds

2 teaspoons vegetable oil

1. Combine water, butter and molasses in small saucepan; heat over low heat to 120°F. Combine 1¼ cups all-purpose flour, rye flour, milk powder, yeast, salt and caraway seeds in large bowl of stand mixer. Slowly add water mixture; beat with paddle attachment at low speed to form soft, sticky dough.

2. Replace paddle attachment with dough hook. Gradually add enough additional all-purpose flour, about ¾ cup, to form rough dough. Add remaining flour, 1 tablespoon at a time, if necessary to prevent sticking. Mix at low speed 5 minutes or until dough is smooth and elastic.

3. Shape dough into a ball. Place in greased bowl; turn to grease top. Cover and let rise in warm place 35 to 40 minutes or until dough has increased in size by one third.

4. Spray 8- or 9-inch round cake pan with nonstick cooking spray. Punch down dough. Divide dough in half; roll each half into 12-inch log. Cut each log into 12 pieces with sharp knife; shape each piece into a tight ball. Place balls in single layer in prepared pan; brush with oil. Cover loosely with lightly greased sheet of plastic wrap and let rise in warm place 45 minutes or until doubled in size. Preheat oven to 375°F.

5. Bake 15 to 20 minutes or until rolls are golden brown. Cool in pan 5 minutes; remove to wire rack to cool completely.

Baked Doughnuts with Cinnamon Glaze

Makes 24 doughnuts and holes

2 cups milk, divided

½ cup (1 stick) butter

5 to 5½ cups all-purpose flour, divided

⅔ cup granulated sugar

2 packages (¼ ounce each) active dry yeast

1 teaspoon salt

1 teaspoon grated lemon peel

½ teaspoon ground nutmeg

2 eggs

2 cups sifted powdered sugar

½ teaspoon ground cinnamon

1. Combine 1¾ cups milk and butter in medium saucepan; heat over low heat to 120° to 130°F (butter does not need to melt completely). Combine 2 cups flour, granulated sugar, yeast, salt, lemon peel and nutmeg in large bowl of stand mixer. Slowly add milk mixture; beat with paddle attachment at low speed until blended. Beat at medium speed 2 minutes. Beat in eggs and 1 cup flour at low speed. Beat at medium speed 2 minutes.

2. Replace paddle attachment with dough hook. Add enough additional flour, about 2 cups; mix at low speed to form soft dough. Mix 3 minutes, adding remaining flour, 1 tablespoon at at time, if necessary to prevent sticking. Shape dough into a ball. Place dough in greased bowl; turn to grease top. Cover and refrigerate at least 2 hours or up to 24 hours.

3. Punch down dough; turn out onto lightly floured surface. Knead about 1 minute or until no longer sticky. Add enough remaining flour, 1 tablespoon at a time, if necessary to prevent sticking.

4. Line two baking sheets with parchment paper. Roll out dough to ½-inch thickness with lightly floured rolling pin. Cut out dough with floured 2½-inch doughnut cutter. Reroll scraps, reserving doughnut holes. Place doughnuts and holes 2 inches apart on prepared baking sheets. Cover and let rise in warm place about 30 minutes or until doubled in size.

5. For glaze, combine powdered sugar and cinnamon in small bowl; mix well. Stir in remaining milk, 1 tablespoon at at time, until glaze reaches desired consistency. Preheat oven to 400°F.

6. Bake doughnuts and holes 8 to 10 minutes or until golden brown. Remove to wire racks to cool 5 minutes. Place pieces of waxed paper under racks. Dip warm doughnuts into glaze; return to racks to set. Serve warm.

Dinner Rolls

Makes 24 rolls

1¼ **cups milk**

½ **cup shortening**

3¾ **to 4¼ cups all-purpose flour, divided**

¼ **cup sugar**

2 **packages (¼ ounce each) active dry yeast**

1 **teaspoon salt**

2 **eggs**

1. Combine milk and shortening in small saucepan; heat over low heat to 110° to 120°F (shortening does not need to melt completely).

2. Combine 1½ cups flour, sugar, yeast and salt in large bowl of stand mixer. Slowly add milk mixture; beat with paddle attachment at low speed until well blended. Add eggs and 1 cup flour; beat at medium speed 2 minutes. Beat in enough additional flour, about 1¼ cups, to form soft dough.

3. Replace paddle attachment with dough hook. Add remaining flour, 1 tablespoon at a time, if necessary to prevent sticking; mix at low speed 5 to 7 minutes or until dough is smooth and elastic.

4. Shape dough into a ball. Place dough in greased bowl; turn to grease top. Cover and let rise in warm place 1 hour or until doubled in size.

5. Punch down dough; knead on lightly floured surface 1 minute. Cover and let rest 10 minutes. Spray two 8-inch square baking pans with nonstick cooking spray. Divide dough in half. Cut one half into 12 pieces; keep remaining half covered with towel. Shape each piece of dough into a ball; place in rows in one prepared pan. Repeat with remaining dough. Cover and let rise in warm place 30 minutes or until doubled in size. Preheat oven to 375°F.

6. Bake 15 to 20 minutes or until golden brown. Remove to wire racks to cool slightly. Serve warm.

Beer Pretzel Rolls

Makes 12 rolls

1¼ cups lager or pale ale,
   at room temperature

3 tablespoons packed
   brown sugar

2 tablespoons milk

2 tablespoons butter,
   melted

1 package (¼ ounce)
   instant yeast

3 to 4 cups bread flour,
   divided

2 teaspoons salt

4 quarts water

½ cup baking soda

2 teaspoons coarse salt

1. Combine lager, brown sugar, milk, butter and yeast in large bowl of stand mixer. Add 1 cup flour and 2 teaspoons salt; beat with paddle attachment at low speed 2 minutes.

2. Replace paddle attachment with dough hook. Add enough remaining flour, ½ cup at a time, to form stiff dough that cleans side of bowl. Mix at low speed about 5 minutes or until dough is smooth and elastic. Place dough in greased bowl; turn to grease top. Cover and let rise in warm place 1 hour or until doubled in size.

3. Turn out dough onto lightly floured surface; knead several times. Divide dough into 12 pieces; shape each piece into a smooth ball by gently pulling top surface to underside and pinching bottom to seal. Place on ungreased baking sheet. Cover and let rise in warm place 30 minutes or until doubled in size.

4. Position oven rack in center of oven. Preheat oven to 425°F. Line second baking sheet with parchment paper.

5. Bring water and baking soda to a boil in large saucepan over high heat. Add rolls to water, a few at a time; cook until puffed, turning once. Drain rolls on clean kitchen towel; place 2 inches apart on prepared baking sheet. Cut 1½-inch "X" in top of each roll with kitchen scissors. Sprinkle with coarse salt.

6. Bake 15 to 18 minutes or until rolls are crisp and brown. Remove to wire rack to cool slightly.

Egg Bagels

Makes 12 bagels

1 package (¼ ounce)
   active dry yeast

2 tablespoons plus
   1 teaspoon sugar, divided

½ to ¾ cup warm water
   (105° to 115°F), divided

2½ cups all-purpose flour

1 tablespoon vegetable oil

1 teaspoon salt

2 eggs

2 quarts water

2 tablespoons cold water

1. Dissolve yeast and 1 teaspoon sugar in ¼ cup warm water in small bowl; let stand 5 minutes or until bubbly.

2. Combine flour, oil and salt in food processor; process 5 seconds or just until blended. Add yeast mixture and 1 egg; process 10 seconds or until blended. With motor running, slowly drizzle just enough warm water through feed tube until dough forms a ball. Process until ball turns around bowl about 25 times. Let dough rest 1 to 2 minutes.

3. With motor running, slowly drizzle in enough remaining warm water to make dough soft, smooth and satiny. Process until dough turns around bowl about 15 times. Shape dough into a ball. Place in greased bowl; turn to grease top. Cover and let rise 15 minutes.

4. Line baking sheets with parchment paper. Divide dough into 12 pieces; roll each piece into 6-inch rope. Bring both ends of each piece together to form circle; moisten ends and pinch together to seal. Place on prepared baking sheets; let rest 15 minutes.

5. Combine 2 quarts water and remaining 2 tablespoons sugar in large saucepan or Dutch oven; bring to a boil over medium-high heat. Working in batches, gently lower bagels into boiling water. When they rise to the surface, turn and cook 2 minutes or until puffy. Use slotted spoon to remove bagels from water; return to baking sheets.

6. Preheat oven to 425°F. Beat remaining egg and 2 tablespoons cold water in small bowl. Brush over bagels.

7. Bake 20 to 25 minutes or until crusts are golden brown and crisp. Remove to wire racks to cool.

Sour Cream and Onion Rolls

Makes 12 rolls

1 tablespoon butter

1 cup chopped onion, divided

3¼ cups all-purpose flour, divided

1 package (¼ ounce) instant yeast

1 tablespoon sugar

1 teaspoon salt

1 cup warm beer (120°F)

½ cup sour cream

2 tablespoons butter, melted

1. Spray 10-inch pie plate with nonstick cooking spray. Melt 1 tablespoon butter in small skillet over medium-high heat. Add ¼ cup onion; cook and stir 3 to 4 minutes or until tender.

2. Combine 2 cups flour, yeast, sugar and salt in large bowl of stand mixer. Add warm beer; beat with paddle attachment at low speed until blended. Add sour cream; beat at medium-high speed 2 minutes.

3. Replace paddle attachment with dough hook. Add ½ cup onion; mix until incorporated. Add enough remaining flour, ¼ cup at a time, to form soft dough. Mix at low speed 3 minutes or until dough is smooth and elastic.

4. Shape dough into 12 balls with greased hands. Smooth tops of balls; place in prepared pie plate. Cover loosely and let rise in warm place 20 minutes.

5. Preheat oven to 400°F. Brush tops with melted butter; sprinkle with remaining ¼ cup onion.

6. Bake 25 to 30 minutes or until lightly browned. Cool in pan on wire rack 5 minutes. Serve warm or at room temperature.

Jelly Doughnut Bites

Makes 48 doughnut bites

1¼ teaspoons active
    dry yeast

½ cup plus 3 tablespoons
    warm milk (95° to
    105°F), divided

⅓ cup granulated sugar

1 tablespoon butter,
    softened

2½ to 2¾ cups all-purpose
    flour

1 egg

½ teaspoon salt

½ cup raspberry jam

    Powdered sugar

1. Dissolve yeast in 3 tablespoons warm milk in large bowl of stand mixer; let stand 5 minutes or until bubbly. Add granulated sugar, butter and remaining ½ cup milk; beat with paddle attachment at medium speed until blended.

2. Replace paddle attachment with dough hook. Add 2¼ cups flour, egg and salt; mix at low speed until dough begins to climb up dough hook. Add enough remaining flour, 1 tablespoon at a time, if necessary to prevent sticking. Mix at low speed 3 minutes or until dough is smooth and elastic.

3. Shape dough into a ball. Place dough in greased bowl; turn to grease top. Cover and let rise in warm place 1 hour or until doubled in size.

4. Spray 48 mini (1¾-inch) muffin cups with nonstick cooking spray. Punch down dough. Shape pieces of dough into 1-inch balls; place in prepared muffin cups. Cover and let rise 1 hour. Preheat oven to 375°F.

5. Bake 10 to 12 minutes or until light golden brown. Remove to wire racks to cool completely.

6. Place jam in pastry bag fitted with small round tip. Insert tip into side of each doughnut; squeeze about 1 teaspoon jam into center. Sprinkle filled doughnuts with powdered sugar.

Tip: These doughnuts are best eaten the same day they are made. They can be served warm or at room temperature. If desired, microwave on HIGH 10 seconds just before serving.

Prosciutto Provolone Rolls

Makes 12 rolls

3 cups all-purpose flour,
   divided

1 package (¼ ounce)
   instant yeast

1½ teaspoons salt

1 cup warm water (120°F)

2 tablespoons olive oil

⅓ cup garlic and herb
   spreadable cheese

6 thin slices prosciutto
   (3-ounce package)

6 slices (1 ounce each)
   provolone cheese

1. Combine 1½ cups flour, yeast and salt in large bowl of stand mixer. Add warm water and oil; beat with paddle attachment at medium speed 2 minutes.

2. Replace paddle attachment with dough hook. Add remaining 1½ cups flour; mix at low speed 2 minutes to form soft dough that cleans side of bowl. Mix at low speed 6 to 8 minutes or until dough is smooth and elastic.

3. Shape dough into a ball. Place dough in greased bowl; turn to grease top. Cover and let rise in warm place about 30 minutes or until doubled in size.

4. Punch down dough. Spray 12 standard (2½-inch) muffin cups with nonstick cooking spray.

5. Roll out dough into 12×10-inch rectangle on lightly floured surface. Spread garlic and herb cheese evenly over dough; top with prosciutto and provolone slices. Starting with long side, roll up dough jelly-roll style; pinch seam to seal. Cut crosswise into 1-inch slices; arrange slices, cut sides up, in prepared muffin cups. Cover and let rise in warm place about 25 minutes or until almost doubled in size. Preheat oven to 375°F.

6. Bake about 20 minutes or until golden brown. Loosen edges of rolls with knife; remove to wire rack. Serve warm.

Soft Pretzel Bites

Makes 12 servings

1 package (¼ ounce)
active dry yeast

2 teaspoons sugar

½ teaspoon salt

1⅔ cups warm water
(105° to 115°F)

4½ cups all-purpose flour

2 tablespoons butter,
softened

12 cups water

½ cup baking soda

Coarse salt (optional)

Honey mustard (optional)

1. Dissolve yeast, sugar and ½ teaspoon salt in 1⅔ cups warm water in large bowl of stand mixer; let stand 5 minutes or until bubbly.

2. Add flour and butter; beat with paddle attachment at low speed until combined, scraping side of bowl occasionally. Replace paddle attachment with dough hook; mix at medium speed 5 minutes. (If dough wraps around hook, remove dough, place at bottom of bowl and resume mixing.)

3. Shape dough into a ball. Place dough in greased bowl; turn to grease top. Cover and let rise in warm place 1 hour or until doubled in size.

4. Preheat oven to 450°F. Line baking sheets with foil; spray foil with nonstick cooking spray. Punch down dough; turn out onto floured surface. Divide dough into 12 pieces. Flatten and stretch each piece of dough; roll into 12-inch-long rope. Cut each rope into eight equal pieces.

5. Bring 12 cups water to a boil in large saucepan over medium-high heat; stir in baking soda until dissolved. Working in batches, drop dough pieces into boiling water; boil 30 seconds. Use slotted spoon to remove dough to prepared baking sheets. Sprinkle with coarse salt, if desired.

6. Bake 12 minutes or until dark golden brown, rotating baking sheets halfway through. Serve with honey mustard, if desired.

Italian Pull-Apart Rolls

Makes 15 rolls

3¾ cups bread flour, divided

1½ tablespoons sugar

1 package (¼ ounce) instant yeast

1½ teaspoons salt

¾ cup warm water (120°F)

½ cup warm milk (120°F)

2 tablespoons olive oil

¾ cup grated Parmesan cheese

2 teaspoons Italian seasoning

⅓ cup butter, melted

1. Combine 1½ cups flour, sugar, yeast and salt in large bowl of stand mixer. Add warm water, warm milk and oil; beat with paddle attachment at medium speed 3 minutes.

2. Replace paddle attachment with dough hook. Add 2 cups flour; mix at low speed to form firm dough. Add enough remaining flour, 1 tablespoon at a time, if necessary to prevent sticking. Mix at low speed 5 minutes.

3. Shape dough into a ball. Place dough in greased bowl; turn to grease top. Cover and let rise in warm place about 30 minutes or until doubled in size.

4. Spray 2½-quart baking dish with nonstick cooking spray. Combine cheese and Italian seasoning in shallow bowl. Place melted butter in another shallow bowl.

5. Turn out dough onto lightly floured surface; roll gently into 20-inch rope. Divide dough into 15 pieces; roll each piece into a ball. Dip balls in melted butter; roll in cheese mixture to coat. Place in prepared baking dish; cover and let rise about 30 minutes or until doubled in size. Preheat oven to 375°F.

6. Bake about 30 minutes or until rolls are golden brown. Cool in pan on wire rack 10 minutes. Serve warm.

Garlic Knots

Makes 20 knots

1 package (¼ ounce) active dry yeast	4 tablespoons (½ stick) butter, divided
1 teaspoon sugar	1 tablespoon minced garlic
¾ cup warm water (105° to 115°F)	¼ teaspoon garlic powder
2¼ cups all-purpose flour	½ cup grated Parmesan cheese
2 tablespoons olive oil, divided	2 tablespoons chopped fresh parsley
1½ teaspoons salt, divided	½ teaspoon dried oregano

1. Dissolve yeast and sugar in warm water in large bowl of stand mixer; let stand 5 minutes or until bubbly. Add flour, 1 tablespoon oil and 1 teaspoon salt; mix with dough hook at low speed 5 minutes or until dough is smooth and elastic.

2. Shape dough into a ball. Place in large greased bowl; turn to grease top. Cover and let rise in warm place 1 hour or until doubled in size.

3. Melt 2 tablespoons butter in small saucepan over low heat. Add remaining 1 tablespoon oil, ½ teaspoon salt, minced garlic and garlic powder; cook over very low heat 5 minutes. Pour into small bowl; set aside.

4. Preheat oven to 400°F. Line baking sheet with parchment paper.

5. Punch down dough. Turn out dough onto lightly floured surface; let rest 10 minutes. Roll out dough into 10×8-inch rectangle; cut into 20 (2-inch) squares. Roll each piece into 8-inch rope; tie in a knot. Place knots on prepared baking sheet; brush with butter mixture.

6. Bake 10 minutes or until lightly browned. Meanwhile, melt remaining 2 tablespoons butter. Combine cheese, parsley and oregano in small bowl; mix well. Brush melted butter over knots immediately after baking; sprinkle with cheese mixture. Cool slightly; serve warm.

Metric Conversion Chart

VOLUME MEASUREMENTS (dry)

1/8 teaspoon = 0.5 mL
1/4 teaspoon = 1 mL
1/2 teaspoon = 2 mL
3/4 teaspoon = 4 mL
1 teaspoon = 5 mL
1 tablespoon = 15 mL
2 tablespoons = 30 mL
1/4 cup = 60 mL
1/3 cup = 75 mL
1/2 cup = 125 mL
2/3 cup = 150 mL
3/4 cup = 175 mL
1 cup = 250 mL
2 cups = 1 pint = 500 mL
3 cups = 750 mL
4 cups = 1 quart = 1 L

VOLUME MEASUREMENTS (fluid)

1 fluid ounce (2 tablespoons) = 30 mL
4 fluid ounces (1/2 cup) = 125 mL
8 fluid ounces (1 cup) = 250 mL
12 fluid ounces (1 1/2 cups) = 375 mL
16 fluid ounces (2 cups) = 500 mL

WEIGHTS (mass)

1/2 ounce = 15 g
1 ounce = 30 g
3 ounces = 90 g
4 ounces = 120 g
8 ounces = 225 g
10 ounces = 285 g
12 ounces = 360 g
16 ounces = 1 pound = 450 g

DIMENSIONS

1/16 inch = 2 mm
1/8 inch = 3 mm
1/4 inch = 6 mm
1/2 inch = 1.5 cm
3/4 inch = 2 cm
1 inch = 2.5 cm

OVEN TEMPERATURES

250°F = 120°C
275°F = 140°C
300°F = 150°C
325°F = 160°C
350°F = 180°C
375°F = 190°C
400°F = 200°C
425°F = 220°C
450°F = 230°C

BAKING PAN SIZES

Utensil	Size in Inches/Quarts	Metric Volume	Size in Centimeters
Baking or Cake Pan (square or rectangular)	8×8×2	2 L	20×20×5
	9×9×2	2.5 L	23×23×5
	12×8×2	3 L	30×20×5
	13×9×2	3.5 L	33×23×5
Loaf Pan	8×4×3	1.5 L	20×10×7
	9×5×3	2 L	23×13×7
Round Layer Cake Pan	8×1½	1.2 L	20×4
	9×1½	1.5 L	23×4
Pie Plate	8×1¼	750 mL	20×3
	9×1¼	1 L	23×3
Baking Dish or Casserole	1 quart	1 L	—
	1½ quart	1.5 L	—
	2 quart	2 L	—